PRETTY NEAT

the buttoned-up way to get organized & let go of perfection

ALICIA ROCKMORE & SARAH WELCH
Cofounders and Creators of buttoned up® *Inc. and Products*

SEAL PRESS

PRETTY NEAT

The Buttoned-Up Way to Get Organized and Let Go of Perfection

Copyright © 2010 by Alicia Rockmore & Sarah Welch

Published by
Seal Press
A Member of the Perseus Books Group
1700 Fourth Street
Berkeley, California

Library of Congress Cataloging-in-Publication Data

Rockmore, Alicia.
  Pretty neat : the buttoned-up way to get organized and let go of perfection / Alicia Rockmore and Sarah Welch.
     p. cm.
  ISBN 978-1-58005-309-9
  1. Time management. 2. Orderliness. I. Welch, Sarah. II. Title.
  BF637.T5R63 2010
  640--dc22
                              2010008518

Cover and interior design by Kate Basart/Union Pageworks
Printed in the United States of America by Edwards Brothers
Distributed by Publishers Group West

CONTENTS

For Gardiner, William, and Lachlan—I love you infinity.

—SARAH

For Adam, who is always there and supports me in everything I do.

To Lucy, who is the shining light in my life and an amazing young girl.

I love you both so much!

—ALICIA

ACKNOWLEDGMENTS

This book would not have been possible without input and participation from hundreds of women who took time out of their busy days to talk with us about their overall approach to getting organized and share their best organizational shortcuts. To each and every one of you: please accept our deepest gratitude. We learned so much from you. We hope that we have adequately captured your wisdom in this book. The research for this book was buoyed by the assistance of Anne Marie Furie, our indefatigable "Chief Juggler" at Buttoned Up. Her incredible interview skills and ability to help us organize the information collected made it easy to find and distill the insights, and her eagle eye helped us clean up our writing style. We owe Leah Ticker a special thanks for her dedicated hard work. The rest of the amazing Buttoned Up team cheered us on and kept us going when we were tired and cranky: Hollie, Nancy, Susan, and Gina—we would be lost without you. Jane Dystel, our agent, provided wonderful advice throughout the process. Krista Lyons, our editor, looked at our manuscript with a fresh and seasoned eye, making many valuable suggestions. We could not have completed the book without the support of our families. They gave us the time we needed to work on the manuscript, including the occasional late night and weekend, and encouraged us when we needed a boost. Thank you from the bottom of our hearts Gardiner, William, Lachlan, Adam, and Lucy. And finally, we owe a special thanks to the special women in our lives. Your friendship, support, and love mean so very much to us, and your wisdom made this book better. Thank you to Alison Lord, Liz Gruzkievicz, Amy Stanton, Kerry Lyons, Ann Taylor, Maggie Ferguson, Kate Hosford, Lindsey Welch, Libby Welch, Zeyna Ballee, Michelle Michilini, Cyndi Manzo, Liz Paley, Angela Harris, Pam Werner, Amy Lerner Hill, Marci Miller, Kim Lerner, Hope Wintner, Jodie Schroeder, Susie Stein, Carrie Neustadt, and Aimee Sesar.

INTRODUCTION: ORG PORN

Negative self-image. Fantasy-induced overspending. Marital tension. A new kind of airbrushed concoction is wreaking havoc on our homes and our psyches: a little something we like to call "org porn." What is it? Well, we define org porn as that glossy, airbrushed fantasy world where everything is pristine, serene, and perfectly in order, sort of like *Playboy*, but with chore charts and name-plated cubbyholes. It's everywhere you look these days: in magazines, coffee table books, advertisements, and TV shows. And when consumed in excess, it can lead to feelings of inadequacy, binge spending on organizational products, and even marital discord. We have interviewed hundreds of women on the topic of organization and an astounding 80 percent of them feel they fall well short of the mark when it comes to getting organized.

Don't get us wrong, gazing at beautiful images of meticulously organized rooms, perfectly displayed collections, color-coordinated closets, flawless family schedules, pristine kitchens, tidy mud rooms, and picture-perfect work spaces can be titillating. There's a reason we call it org porn! But when it becomes the primary standard by which you measure your own general state of organization, it is unhealthy. An airbrushed land of perfect organization cannot be sustained in this messy, unpredictable world called real life.

Chasing perfection fuels something we call "organizational inertia," a type of paralysis that makes it virtually impossible to get started. All too often, the most difficult part of getting organized is knowing where to start. If perfection is the objective, that paralysis makes sense. Keeping your house, work, and schedule magazine-ready requires a superhuman effort to achieve and constant superhuman vigilance to maintain. The goal of getting organized isn't necessarily to have everything picture-perfect, but rather to eliminate inefficiency so that you have more time to do what you actually want to do.

Instead of holding yourself to an impossible org-porn standard, we advocate ditching perfection and instead focusing on why you want to get organized in the first place. Remind yourself that org porn is merely entertainment and an escape that few, if any, actually achieve. If it helps you, use those org-porn images to focus on the benefits you are trying to achieve: calm, efficiency, etc. Once you are clear on the real objective, then you are free to define your own rules for achieving that goal (and what that will look like for you).

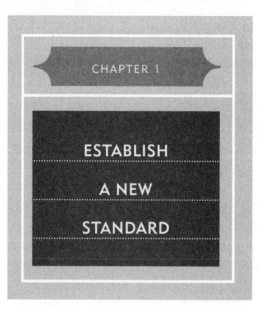

CHAPTER 1

ESTABLISH
A NEW
STANDARD

"The thing that is really hard, and really amazing, is giving up on

being perfect and beginning the work of becoming yourself."

—ANNA QUINDLEN

Rosemary Biagioni has a cherubic face, sparkling eyes, and a zest for life. She works full time as a finance director for a start-up in New York, runs a household single-handedly, and somehow never misses a beat in the lives of her two sons, Sergio and Nicholas. Interestingly, she only considers herself moderately organized.

She's not alone.

Cindi Leive, the glamorous-in-a-totally-approachable-way editor in chief of *Glamour* magazine, juggles a lot: a high-octane job, motherhood, marriage, friends, family, and charity work. When we asked her if she'd be willing to be interviewed for this book, Cindi noted wryly, "I'm not sure I can contribute anything useful. I think I might be more of an organizational 'before,' than an 'after.'"

We heard the same thing from women everywhere we went: "I wouldn't really consider myself super organized. Are you sure you want to talk to me?" Angela Harris, busy mom of two, joked, "People think I'm organized because I juggle things. But my car, my gym locker, and my office tell the real story."

Even those who described themselves as very organized, even anal, were quick to point out their flaws and shortcomings. None felt remotely qualified to have their organizational tricks held up as examples of what to do.

Why on earth, we asked ourselves, did these women feel their "imperfect" ways left them short of the mark organizationally? Perhaps it's because perfection has been held up as the gold standard when it comes to organization. We think it's high time for a new standard of organization: an *im*perfect one.

What does it mean to be imperfectly organized? Foremost, it is a mindset. It means making a conscious decision to let go of the notion that everything must pass inspection by the organizational police, and instead permit yourself to keep the gears of your life turning in your own unique way. Even if it involves shortcuts and a little messiness that might horrify your mother or mother-in-law, the goal is to have enough structure in place to avoid missing important things, yet remain limber enough to handle the inevitable curveballs that get thrown your way. And unless you have enough time to make

PRETTY NEAT WISDOM

As you read this book and begin to formulate your own definition of successful imperfection, keep these questions in mind:

- Do I feel at peace when I think about the activities and belongings in my life?
- Do I waste energy worrying about things that might not get done?
- What am I sacrificing in order to complete a particular task? Time? Money?
- Why is it important to get this done?
- How would I feel tomorrow if this task was still not completed? A week from now? Six months from now? Why do I feel this way?

When it comes to getting organized, there is only one thing that matters: your own sense of having it together. Focus on defining what that means to you.

organization a full-time job, you'll need to embrace shortcuts and imperfect approaches to getting organized. Remember, organization is not an end state, it's an ongoing fact of life—a process. Color-coded family schedules, name-plated toy cubbies, and pristine closets are nice to have and even nicer to look at in books and magazines. But if you don't have them, it doesn't mean you're not truly organized. Imperfect approaches to organization work. The tips we've collected are straightforward enough to be useful to almost everybody. And even better, they've been road tested for effectiveness.

EMBRACE INTELLIGENT SHORTCUTS

In spite of protestations to the contrary, we were sure that women like Cindi, Rosemary, and Angela used a great deal of intelligence in their approaches, however haphazard those might appear. How else could they be leading such rich, full lives? We had a hunch that, at least subliminally, they and the hundreds of other women we interviewed had embraced the concept of *imperfect organization*. In other words, they knew which organizational battles were worth fighting and how to shortcut their way to success. As Rosemary puts it, "I just try to live by the credo, 'Don't major in the minors.'"

Person after person we spoke with had novel yet highly effective ways to cut organizational corners, saving precious time and energy. A lot of people were sheepish about the imperfect nature of their solutions. But while they often traded picture-perfect outcomes for functionality, their imperfect ways of getting things organized were anything but short of the mark. Here is a sampling of great ideas we heard from people like you.

A Pretty Neat Tip

SUSAN'S TRUSTY TAX FILE

When it comes to filing complex things, like tax prep stuff, accountant Susan Bachtelle has an imperfect system that seems to work perfectly. "I think there's a tendency to over-filing, which can actually cost you more time in the long run. I have one hanging file for tax documents, with two manila subfolders: one for income/expenses and another for deductions. I put the hanging file in the very front of the filing cabinet so that it's the first thing I hit when I open it. That makes it easy for me to throw my receipts into the appropriate folder throughout the year. It's so easy to deal with, I don't procrastinate on filing. Then at the end of the year, I'm set."

MAY'S HUTCH CRUTCH

May Kamalik has a down-and-dirty way of dealing with paper clutter. "I have a hutch desk with a top that closes, so you can't really see what's inside. It's where all the mail and paper clutter get dumped: magazines, mail, coupons, gum—you name it, it goes there. It's a disaster. But I shut the top and it magically disappears. Every Saturday morning, I wake up with a cup of coffee and clean out as much as I can. If it gets to the point where the top won't close, I'll devote a few hours to thoroughly cleaning it out."

ANGELA'S PHOTO FINISH
Angela Harris takes a less than perfect approach to organizing family photos, but it works. "Someday I'll create incredible photo albums; let's be clear that I haven't let go of that fantasy completely. But in the interim, I have created a simple solution, although it's not exactly the most cost-efficient. Everything is digital now, so I order pictures electronically in really big batches—it could be six months to a year's worth of photos at a time. I also order a few easy, slide-in photo albums at the same time. Then, when I'm watching TV, I'll slide photos in and get them done. As I said, it's not cost-effective or particularly beautiful, but I've let go of that. What counts is that we have albums we can pull out and look at."

LIZ'S TOY TRUCE
Liz Gruszkieviz has three children—a toddler and twin nine-year-old girls—the requisite mountain of toys that accompany them, and rudimentary rules for keeping them somewhat corralled. "We have a finished basement, which is where the toys really should be. But you can't really expect kids to confine their play to one area. I keep a big basket in the living room, but it is always overflowing. When it gets really bad, the girls help me schlep everything back downstairs. In addition to the toy baskets upstairs, I have a rule that no new toy can come into the house unless two other toys go out. The only time that gets tough to enforce is birthdays!"

MARCI'S PAPER PILES
Marci Miller gets around her tendency to create piles with something she calls the One Look Rule. "I totally rely on the One Look Rule . . . look at it and then take care of it. Immediately. No ifs, ands, or buts. Because I know if I stick it in a pile, I won't ever get back to it and the pile will just sit there forever, mocking me."

ROSEMARY'S MAIL MANAGER
Rosemary Biagioni long ago gave up the fight against what for many is an Achilles' heel—the daily onslaught of mail. "I can't have mail and stuff like

that cluttering up my counters. That would make me nuts. But it's relentless." Rosemary uses a perfectly *imperfect* approach to dealing with it, but on her terms. "I switched to e-statements for all of my accounts, and I pay all my bills electronically, so I never have to worry about those getting lost in the shuffle. I also put two bins near my front-door mail drop. The first is for magazines and catalogs and the other is for mail. If I see a letter from school, I'll open that immediately. Otherwise, I don't feel guilty about going through the two big baskets only once a month when I have the time and energy to plow through them." Her approach, she admits, is not beautiful, but it works. "Somehow, when it's all contained in those two baskets, it doesn't bother me in the slightest."

MARIE AND EILEEN'S ROOM RESIGNATION

Many moms—particularly those with more than three children—develop a healthy acceptance of their kids' messy rooms. Marie Adele Dennis, mom of six, put it eloquently: "To function well, I really need my space to be orderly. But once my kids were older than two, I was able to accept that their rooms were a total disaster. It was their space. If some of their clutter invaded my space, I didn't argue with them about it. I just put it in their room and closed the door." Eileen Opatut, an outgoing television executive and mother of three, told us, "I grew up in a perfectionist household. Now that I have teenagers, I have a different state of mind—if nothing is growing in their rooms, I just shut the door. The kids are much more willing to clean up, especially if I don't force them. All the mess used to make my blood boil. Now I just let it go."

FIND YOUR INNER AHA!

It is liberating to let go of perfectionist goals that once drained you of energy and goodwill. Amy Hill, mom and full-time lawyer, used to compare herself to her friends, each of whom seemed to juggle a million and one obligations and keep a perfectly organized house without breaking a sweat. That is, until she realized she was being too hard on herself.

"One day, I walked into a friend's house and realized that her *House Beautiful* home was that way in only three rooms. All the toys, junk, and clothes were shoved away behind closed doors in the back part of the house. She wasn't totally together, but she was an expert in hiding the flaws. That was the turning point for me. It was so therapeutic to realize I didn't need to stress anymore over the fact that I wasn't measuring up."

Many women we interviewed have let go of things that used to make them crazy, like imperfectly folded clothes or messy children's rooms. But

Most people think they have to wait for aha moments to come to them. But that's not necessarily the case. You can speed up the process with two exercises.

FILL THIRTY MINUTES A DAY

Imagine you have only thirty minutes a day to get everything done. Grab a sheet of paper and quickly write down what you would do during that half-hour time slot. Don't think about it, just write—make it stream of consciousness. When you are done, examine the list. What is on it? What is *not*? More than likely, this is a fairly complete list of what matters to you and can be the first step in letting go of the rest.

GAIN A NEW PERSPECTIVE

Sometimes, a little distance from a problem is the key to insight. Others in your life may have a better perspective than you on the scope of what you do to stay organized. Interview a few close friends and family members and ask them to step into your shoes. What would their priorities be if they were you? What tasks would they let go of? This very simple exercise may help speed your aha moment of becoming imperfectly organized.

they are often unclear on just *how* they arrived at that aha! moment of realization that they needn't hold themselves to a perfectionist standard. For the majority of women we interviewed, it seemed to have happened gradually and subconsciously. Marci Miller, a lawyer and mom of four children, ages five to thirteen, struggled with feelings of organizational inadequacy. "I never made any progress, and I always felt guilty and bad about myself. I just didn't know where to begin to get everything together. One day, and I'm not sure exactly when, I simply surrendered. It was a turning point, and it felt great not to try to be perfect. I found it was okay to let people see my chaos. My friends, it turns out, are also a lot less organized than I thought they were, and that bonded us together."

Having an aha! moment is a crucial step toward embracing imperfect organization. By "aha!" we mean a moment of insight in which your intellectual and emotional centers simultaneously "get it," enabling you to let go of opposing thoughts that once caused tension and stress (such as, "I'm too busy to get x, y, and z organized, but I'm a failure if I don't get x, y, and z organized"). Aha!'s are the key to change. When you have one, you can let go of previous beliefs that once held you back and adopt new ones that will carry you forward in a more positive way. As a result, you're rewarded with a rush of relief and a general lightness of being.

DEVELOP YOUR OWN MEANING OF ORGANIZED

Remember Amy Hill, the busy attorney who experienced her aha! moment inside a friend's not-so-*House-Beautiful* home? Her first clue that she needed to redefine her view of organization came when her son, Lincoln, was born. "As a new mom, I couldn't do it all," she admits, "but I had trouble figuring out what to let go of from my old life. It took me a few months, but I realized there were things I could live without, like having a clean car all the time, and things I could not give up, like my workouts. It was a bit of trial and error, but over time I got there. My list is not static. If I have a trial to prepare for, things fall by the wayside for a few weeks. That's okay because I get to the important things eventually."

You certainly don't need to wait for a major life event like having a child to reevaluate your own definition of organized, but you do need to take a structured approach. Our goal in this section is to help you define it in a way that will enable you to do a better job of managing the things you love to do, not do more organizing. Taking charge may feel strange at first—old habits die hard. But it is worth the effort. It's tempting to define organizational solutions tactically, such as "set up a filing system" or "get toy bins." But unless you take the time to (1) identify your real organizational issues, (2) understand the root causes of those issues, and (3) consciously arrive at a clear understanding of a "good enough" goal, you're likely to fall back into your old habits. Take a few minutes to do the three exercises below, which are designed to help you do just that.

IDENTIFY YOUR PROBLEM AREAS

Think about the way you organize the important things in your life. What works well for you? What needs just a small tune-up? What needs a complete overhaul? Write your answers in a list like this.

Example:

RUNNING WELL	NEEDS A TUNE-UP	NEEDS AN OVERHAUL
Meals	Office	Personal time

IDENTIFY YOUR SHOULD-DO PROBLEM

For each of the areas you listed under either the Needs a Tune-Up or Needs an Overhaul column, take a moment to articulate what you think being organized should look like. "Shoulds" are, by definition, part of your problem; the very word *should* implies that someone has expectations of you.

Understanding that you are working to someone else's standard can be illuminating. Consider where that *should* came from. Your mom? Images of others' homes? Magazines?

Example:

AREA	I SHOULD BE DOING / IT SHOULD LOOK LIKE	ORIGIN OF SHOULD
Office	No papers on the desk, important things filed away, pens and pencils in holder, books in bookshelf next to desk vs. on desk.	Mom, my fantasy (probably inspired by org porn)

ESTABLISH YOUR GOOD ENOUGH GOALS

Now, take a deep breath, accept that life is messy and unpredictable, and embrace your vision of imperfect organization. For each of these areas, outline what you *really* need to do (versus what you think you should do) for a problem area to cease being a problem. While you're at it, outline some actions that can help you attain that good enough goal.

Example:

AREA	GOOD ENOUGH GOAL	TACTICS
Desk	Once a month give it a clean slate.	Set a recurring 45-minute appointment in your calendar for the second Thursday of every month. Use that time to give your desk a clean slate.

Once you have set your good enough goals, do not apologize to anyone for the shortcuts you take or the chores that might not get done.

PREPARE YOURSELF FOR IMPERFECTION

Just because you've decided to let something go intellectually doesn't mean it will be easy. Take Rebecca Saliman, for example, a hyperorganized middle school teacher from Los Angeles who grew up in an immaculate home. When she moved out on her own, she instinctively adopted her mother's definition of organization.

"From when I was a little kid, my mom taught me that everything had to have a home," she explained. "Our house was so orderly, no item was ever 'homeless.' She was famous for tossing the newspaper before any of us kids had even rolled out of bed. I remember spending many Sunday mornings digging through the trash bin looking for the comics. Gross! Back then, it definitely felt like my mom was extreme, but now that I'm an adult, I find myself behaving the exact same way without even thinking about it!"

Although she admits it wasn't easy, Rebecca learned to let some things go and is beginning to accept organizational imperfection on her own terms. "Papers are a huge pet peeve of mine, but here I am in my home office, staring at a thick pile of paperwork just begging to be filed. I see it, and I say, 'I'm a teacher, and summer will be here soon.' Instead of obsessing about the massive pile, I can work on more important things, like tomorrow's lesson plan."

Rebecca does two things well. First, she has a mantra. Every time she looks at the pile, she says to herself, "Pile, I see you, and I am ignoring you for now." It's a conscious decision on her part, one that acknowledges there is a problem that will be addressed at a later date. The second thing she does well is set a time line: "I have a summer to-do list and that pile is on the list. I tell myself, 'summer will be here soon,' and I mean it. If I were ignoring it forever, that would stress me out, but if I know it will get done in the near future, then it's fine with me."

Overcoming the perfectionist model you learned as a child isn't easy, and there will always be a voice—whether it's your own or somebody else's—pointing out the flaws in your approach. The trick to sticking to your plan without guilt or feelings of inadequacy is to own the imperfections in your approach. That requires a little advance planning.

A Pretty Neat Tip

TIME IS MONEY

Once you start embracing imperfection you will find that certain things may still try to claw their way back on to your to-do list. Reward yourself for making progress. Get a glass jar with a lid and each time you resist the urge to do something you have agreed to let go of, put a dollar in the jar. After a few weeks, use the money in the jar to reward yourself. It is a simple but important reminder that by embracing imperfection and NOT doing something, you are saving yourself time, and time is money.

PREPARE REBUTTALS IN ADVANCE

We often struggle with accepting an imperfect mind-set because we are afraid of what others will think of us. They may think we are not good mothers, wives, or women if we suddenly stop striving for perfection. We need to stop doing things for others, believe in who we are, and let go of the devil on our shoulders. This is very simple to do.

Meet: Juju Chang

Family: Married mother of three

Occupation: Anchor, ABC News, *Good Morning America*

Q: What does "being organized" mean to you?

A: Well, my whole life is what I like to call organized chaos, and that's best represented by the little piles that are all over my house (not just my desk). I have one pile of bills; some paid, some waiting to be paid. Another pile of school forms; some finished, others not. And so on. I put sticky notes on them with the deadline so I know when I have to get it done by, and as long as I'm not late, I consider myself to be organized.

Q: You are such a champion of the "imperfect" on GMA. It sounds like you're that way when it comes to organization too, which is great. What was your aha! moment?

A: I wasn't always comfortable with imperfection. I was always the kid who needed to be graded. I was the one striving for that "A," first in school, and then later I transferred that to my work. But in real life, there is no one grading you but *you*. I was actually having one of those "need to be graded" moments, where I was questioning who I was and what I was doing (Should I stay at home? Should I work more? Should, should, should) when I had the aha! I happened to be in the back of a taxi, and it stopped in front of a church. There was a little quote by Annie Dillard in the bulletin board out front that said: "The way you spend your day is of course the way you spend your life." I thought to myself—that's it! Now when I hear those "shoulds" enter my mind, I try to look at whatever I'm doing in the moment within the context of the big picture: Is this how I want to spend my day/my life? If not, it's easier to let it go.

Q: What kind of organizational shortcuts do you take?

A: My piles and sticky notes are definitely one. Another big one is related to time. My new job requires that I be in the office early in the morning. I remember struggling with the thought of never doing school drop-off again. But rather than looking at it as an either/or thing, I chose yes/and. Now I Skype with my kids while I'm in my dressing room. I have them up and we literally eat breakfast together and discuss what to expect for the day. It would work for any mom who's traveling too. I've also made an effort to be less of a perfectionist at work, which to me is my biggest shortcut.

Write down your three biggest critics (e.g., mom, mother-in-law, spouse, best friend). Then write down three to five organizational tasks you struggle with but do primarily to win their favorable view of you, your home, and your family. For each of the areas you picked, write down what your critics might say if you didn't complete these tasks. Next, write down what your response to them could be.

For example, let's take making the beds every day. If you did not make the beds every day, your mom might say, "How can you possibly let people into your house with the beds unmade? The place is a mess." A potential response might be, "Mom, it may not be how you would do it, but it's how we do it. Besides, we just climb back into them every night anyway. Why take the time to make them up just for show?"

CHAPTER WRAP-UP

In conducting our interviews for this book, we heard the same thing over and over again: "I don't think I can contribute anything. I'm just not organized." Yet, the best ideas came from those people who juggled many balls and, on most days, dropped at least a few. You are not alone. Imperfect organization is running rampant in your town and on your street. Just look around. You'll see you are not alone.

Embracing imperfect organization is a skill—a skill that you will practice over and over again. Get yourself over perfectionist tendencies by imagining what you would do if you had only thirty minutes in a day to get everything done, or by asking others what they think you could let go of. Then develop your own definition of "organized."

Identify your organizational issues—those areas that you feel need an organizational tune-up or overhaul. Understand the root causes of those issues. What do you think you should be doing and where does that thinking come from?

Consciously arrive at a clear understanding of a good enough goal.

At first, changing what you have done for years and letting go of "must do's" is hard. Prepare for the inevitable voices that will point out the flaws in your new definition and approach. Develop rebuttals in advance for people who might make you feel inadequate and reward yourself for sticking to your good enough standards.

Give these methods a try. If you run into roadblocks, you can always come back to these steps and try again.

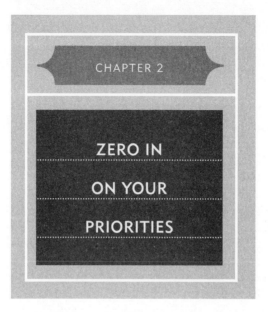

CHAPTER 2

ZERO IN

ON YOUR

PRIORITIES

"The key is not to prioritize what's on your schedule,

but to schedule your priorities."

—STEPHEN R. COVEY

If the Buttoned Up interview crew stopped you on the street right now and asked you to name your top organizational priorities off the top of your head, there's a very good chance you'd be able to do so without too much hemming and hawing. We know because we tried it. We intercepted people in the city centers of Ann Arbor, White Plains, West Hollywood, Nashville, Philadelphia, and New York, in Times Square, and asked that exact question. Ninety-nine percent of the time, people had a very good handle on what they needed to have buttoned up. Yet according to Gallup, sixty percent of Americans between the ages of 18 and 50 feel they have too little time to do what they want in their lives.[1]

So what do your fellow Americans think is most important to have organized? The majority of people we interviewed place the highest priority on the following areas:

- Completing work-related tasks well and on time
- Keeping the home somewhat presentable and functional
- Ensuring finances are in order and bills are paid
- Staying on top of their children's needs and schedules

Indeed, those *do* sound like the right priorities at first blush. But after a few minutes of reflection, the list becomes more interesting for what is *not* on it. For starters, "you" are not anywhere on the list—not your health, not your sanity, not your spirituality, and not your friends or extended family. Another big omission? Long-range planning. And for those in romantic relationships, where's the time to nurture your partnership?

Jeff Anderson, a busy executive and father of four, put it well. "I know that I, personally, am absent from my top three priorities, even though I know taking care of myself is pretty important as well. Unfortunately, it's the first thing to go when the other priorities have to be attended to."

Mother of three Darcy Ahl, who juggles a full-time job and recently launched a start-up, said with some chagrin, "I just looked up and realized that eighteen months have passed since my last ob-gyn visit."

It seems to be a fact of life today that we put ourselves last on the priority list. There's just too much to do and not enough time to do it, so we're often forced to make hard choices, generally under the pressure of immediate deadlines. Everyone we spoke with juggled anywhere from eight to well over twenty tasks on their daily*ish* to-do lists (we say daily*ish* because most people don't make it through their entire lists every day). Most had inventive ways of cutting down their arm-long lists so that they could focus on the most important items. Others fell back on simple approaches. For example, Sally, who juggles a full-time job in banking while taking care of a sick parent, uses what she calls a "sunset" to-do list to help keep herself honest. "The only things that make the list are those tasks that absolutely, positively must be done before the sun sets on any given day." On the other end of the spectrum is Marie Dennis, mother of six and director of a nonprofit. She usually has a lot of lists going. "I organize my thinking by making different kinds of lists. One master list would be too long and too depressing. So for example, I keep one list of things I want to remember when I meet with the leadership team at work, another list of things I have to do in the next day or so, which I keep next to the computer, and a personal list I keep at home next to the fridge or phone. I'll also keep a running list of things I have to write, a list of things I have to give a talk on, etc. Lists just help me focus on what's important and keep me moving in the right direction."

Whatever the mode employed, we found that people who focused a little time on managing their short- and long-term priorities were able to get more done and find a little time for that special someone—you!

WHAT'S DRIVING YOUR TO-DO LIST?

With to-do lists as long as they are, it shouldn't be surprising that deadlines are the number one driver of to-do list action. Not fake ones you use to trick yourself, but real ones with consequences that demand you to follow through.

Eileen Opatut, mom of three teenagers, says, "On a daily basis I have more than a dozen things on my to-do list. On a long-term basis, probably twenty. Some things have a schedule to them, so those are the first things that get done. Say I've got to get my child to her drum lesson, then everything else falls in line behind that."

Hollie Sehrt, a graphic designer juggling two jobs along with a few freelance projects, admits, "I tend to prioritize most often by what's on fire or by what's easy to do in two seconds. For example, if I see an email request for a file come in my inbox, I'll turn that around immediately, so I don't forget to do it later. Longer-range stuff is certainly on my to-do list so I don't forget it, but for the most part, deadlines really drive my agenda."

Ashleigh Sonnenberg admits she procrastinates until she has just enough time to get a task done. "If I know I only have a little time to do it, I will focus up and manage my time a lot better. If I have the luxury of lots of time, I'll try to do a little bit at a time until it's done, but I often end up putting it off until it's closer to the due date and then cramming to complete it."

BethAnn Slater, mom of four who runs a Montessori School, says that during the school year, it's all about putting out fires. "What demands my attention most gets it. But when school is out, I prioritize differently. I do what I feel like and have a little more fun."

THE UPSIDE OF DEADLINE-DRIVEN TO-DO'S

The good news is that deadlines and to-do list overload make it easier to let go of organizational perfection. To navigate her busy agenda, accountant and mother of three Gina Bernstein delineates between public and private spaces. "If I'm the only one that deals with something, like my closet, it's of no consequence to anyone if it's a mess. So getting it organized is a low priority. If it impacts someone else, I put a priority on it."

It took the unexpected arrival of triplets to help Kerry Lyons let go of her desire for picture-perfect organization. "If I look at my life, I can pretty easily divide it into pre-triplets and post-triplets time periods," says Lyons, who also has a four-year old, a two-and-a-half-year-old, and a full-time job. "Pre triplets, if I was hosting a party, I would have felt the need to iron the tablecloth and napkins, put out the right candles, have the perfect flower arrangement on the table, etc. Post triplets, I am happy if I set the table with un-ironed linens and a stack of plates, and let everybody serve themselves. The amazing thing is, nobody has any less of a good time. It never was about the 'look,' but about spending time with people you care about."

For Kate Hosford, graduate school was the trigger that helped her loosen up. "When it comes to organizing, I'm like that children's story *When You Give a Mouse a Cookie.* It goes something like: 'If you give a mouse a cookie, it will probably ask for a glass of milk. If you give a mouse a glass of milk, it will probably ask for a piece of cheese . . . ' and so on. One organizational thing just distracts me to the next. The good thing about school is that my writing can't be pushed to the side. So I manage to ignore a lot of things I don't like to do in order to do my school work, and because I'm paying for school, I feel justified in doing so."

THE DOWNSIDE OF DEADLINE-DRIVEN TO-DO'S

If the good news about to-do-list overload is that it eases perfectionist tendencies, the bad news is that when deadlines drive the bus, things like you, long-range planning, and other important-but-not-yet-on-fire issues take a backseat to the urgent ones. Kim Yorio, a single working mom from Weehawken, New Jersey, illustrates that point. "I have more on my to-do lists than I can possibly get done. I tend to prioritize by deadlines, which means I never get around to organizing something like my will because I don't see my death as imminent. I know I'm taking a risk there, because you never know what will happen."

The other downside of letting deadlines drive your daily to-do list is fatigue. Living a just-in-time life can leave you feeling rushed and frazzled, like you're vaguely behind the eight ball or stuck on a treadmill that's going slightly too fast, to nowhere in particular. In the last chapter, we noted that virtually everyone we interviewed for this book felt to some degree that they were falling short of the organizational mark. Well, we hypothesize that in addition to encouraging unrealistic definitions of organization, a life driven more by deadlines than true priorities contributes to a feeling of organizational inadequacy.

FINDING YOUR FOCUS

Surprisingly, we found only a handful of people who seem to be truly thoughtful about how they select and align their to-do lists with true-life priorities. Make no mistake, these people are under deadline pressures like everybody else, but they are less harried and more confident about their overall level of organization. What separates them from the rest of the pack? They consistently embrace a handful of easy shortcuts to ensure that their daily to-do lists reflect not only what is urgent but also what is important from a long-term perspective.

Virtually every person we talked to had a to-do list longer than they could complete in twenty-four hours. Most people could easily discern what had to get done every day, but critical items such as long-term planning and personal time never made their lists.

We found that people who successfully focus on the day's priorities as well as long-term goals do at least one, and sometimes a combination of, the following:
- Incorporate big picture planning
- Regularly check to-do lists for perspective
- Apply measures of success
- Plan for the unexpected
- Schedule "be you" time

PLAN FOR THE BIG PICTURE

For Jacqueline Jacques, a divorced mom with two young sons, being organized for the short- and long-term is essential. "It's just me and the boys. I work full time and travel extensively and need to coordinate schedules with their dad. Being totally organized is mandatory or things would fall apart. I know that I must look at what needs to get done each day, like sports practice and my work, but I also need to be mindful of what is coming up over the next three or even six months. I cannot be surprised because I have to do it all alone."

Putting a stake in the ground on where your long-term goals lie is critical to setting priorities on a day-to-day basis. Think of it as a yardstick by which to measure your progress against the targets and deadlines you've set for yourself. It may help you decide what priorities matter to you most.

To help set your long-term goals and maintain them on a regular basis, try doing the following: First, every three months schedule one hour into your calendar to think about the long-term goals you want to accomplish. Make a long list of everything you want to get done but have been unable to address. It might be refinancing your mortgage, writing a will, repainting the house, evaluating insurance options, visiting family from out of state . . . the list could go on and on. Take each item and ask yourself two questions: If it is important, why am I not getting to it? And if this was still not done a year from now, would it matter to me?

Now comes the tricky part. Pick only three items to accomplish over the next three months. Setting these longer-term goals and making sure they get on your list of daily to-do's are essential to moving beyond just being a firefighter and instead becoming a good planner.

Take these three big-picture items and determine the steps to accomplishing them. For example, if you want to refinance your mortgage, you might start by calling banks and mortgage brokers to compare rates and terms, then evaluate the costs and benefits of the different options, and so on. This exercise helps you take a monster task and break it into bite-size pieces that are easy to digest. Add them to your daily to-do list and you'll find that you are making progress each week toward your big picture goals. Sound easy? It really is. You'll find that the big hairy goals that once seemed unattainable get done without stress or anxiety. It feels great!

ASK YOUR TO-DO LIST "WHY?"

Most people get into a habit of doing what needs to get done each day and rarely consider whether they're maximizing their time. All of us do this to some degree. It is a coping mechanism that enables us to get done what others expect from us, what is nagging at us, or what keeps us awake at night. We get done what we need to in order to keep our lives and households running smoothly. That said, are you sure, *really sure*, you are doing the most important things on your to-do list each and every day, or are you just putting grease on the squeaky wheel without thinking that you may need a new set of tires instead?

Gardiner Welch, Sarah's husband, has the right idea. "I have a lot on my plate. Every day, or at the very least once a week, I look at what is immediately needed versus the long term; what has to get done today or this week. If I notice that my daily to-do list covers only short-term fires, I try to add in at least one or two items from longer-term projects. In theory, it gives me some balance between the urgent and not-so-urgent-but-important tasks."

To make sure you are focused on the right priorities, you need to understand *why* you are doing things in the first place. Figuring out why doesn't have to be an arduous process. Rather than following your to-do list blindly, set aside five to ten minutes each week to review why each item made the cut. If you are unsure where to start, use the following grid for your list, with 1 being the least important and 10 being the most important:

TASK	IMPORTANT TO ME? RANK FROM 1–10	IMPORTANT TO SOMEONE ELSE? RANK FROM 1–10	WILL DOING THIS MAKE A MEASURABLE DIFFERENCE IN MY WORK OR MY LIFE OVER THE LONG RUN? RANK FROM 1–10

Following this grid will help you identify items with a low importance ranking. Even though a task may be urgent, if you acknowledge that it is unimportant, it is easier to dismiss from your list. To get in the habit of evaluating weekly priorities, schedule time for this review as an appointment every Monday morning.

MEASURE YOUR PROGRESS

What you can *measure* tends to get done. It is a common business principle, one that if applied to your to-do list and big-picture list will help you accomplish what you set out to do. It keeps you honest and on track.

Sarah Merz, President of FranklinCovey, is great at doing just this. "At the beginning of the year, I set a goal that I was going to exercise regularly to reduce my overall stress level and stay healthy. I knew some weeks I'd have more time than others, but I needed to ensure my exercise didn't get pushed to the side in the hectic day-to-day shuffle. So I set a goal that by the end of the year I would run a total of 365 miles. Now I schedule runs in my calendar as if they were appointments. When I complete them, I put a pink dot on the day and pencil in the number of miles I ran. I track my cumulative mileage for the year in the month-at-a-glance section of my agenda. It's a simple way for me to gauge both visually and analytically how I'm tracking. At the

Meet: Sommer Poquette

Family: Married mother of two

Occupation: Early childhood consultant and founder/editor-in-chief of the eco blog GreenandCleanMom.org

Q: Juggling two jobs *and* motherhood can't be easy! Describe your to-do list for us.

A: I actually do not keep a physical to-do list. I'd lose it! In reality, my Blackberry and my calendar function as my list. Between the calendar, with the alarms, and then emails, I really know what I have to get done. Sometimes I will write things down at night before I go to sleep just to get them out of my head. But typically I just follow the calendar, and everything kind of just fits in.

Q: Do you have a to-do list routine?

A: I definitely got in the habit of putting things in my calendar as they come up, which for a lot of things comes via emails. Everything, and I mean *everything*, goes in my calendar: my kids' birthdays, if I have a quarterly report due at work, client phone calls, when my son is responsible for bringing snack to school, etc. Every time I put something in, I will set a reminder for myself, often 12 hours before the "deadline." Those alarms help me plan ahead. I also take a week-long view on Sunday evenings after the kids are in bed. As I'm looking at the calendar for the week ahead, if I think something deadline-driven, like writing an article or a report, is going to take a long time, I block that out. I try to be really realistic as I look at what I have to do in the week ahead and it generally works out well.

Q: How do you decide what gets done and what does not?

A: My deadlines kind of dictate what I have to do. They help me focus. But the way I build deadlines into my calendar really means I've scheduled time for the *work* to get done too. So I can see, well in advance, if I'm going to have a problem. And of

end of every month, I can quickly look back and determine if I am on track or not, and, if need be, make adjustments."

When you set your big picture goals, take the time to create one or two simple milestones to reach along the way and then regularly check in to make sure you are on track. It keeps you honest and helps you focus on achieving your goals.

When Susan Lerner, an empty nester, decided she wanted to make some home improvements to her backyard, she listed two milestones she needed to course, I have a good sense of what my priorities are (family, work, blog) and I'm flexible if I need to be. For example, if my daughter gets sick, I will drop everything that is work- and blog-related and take care of her. Calls, deadlines, etc., that were built in for that day just get shifted to the next day or the next week. I think it's so important to be mentally prepared to be flexible like that. I call it "putting on a new pair of glasses." Sometimes we have pictures in our head of what our life (or schedule) is supposed to look like. But so often, reality doesn't measure up. You have to be ready to adjust and morph to a reality that's different than the picture in your head. Beating yourself up for failing to live up to some perfect picture is a waste of energy. Just snap a new picture or put a different pair of glasses on that lets you see the situation in a new light, and move on.

Q: Where do *you* fit in on your to-do list?

A: Truthfully, I think of the work I do for GreenandCleanMom.org as my "me" time. It's like, if skiing were your hobby and somebody actually *paid* you to do it, you'd be psyched to hit the slopes, right? My hobby is GreenandCleanMom.org. I like the writing, the networking, and all the learning—it's like I'm constantly feeding my brain. I fit that in primarily in the evenings after the kids are in bed and on Sunday afternoons. As far as other things like haircuts, doctor's appointments, etc., I try to fit those in during my lunch hour.

Q: What are your tricks for getting important, but not necessarily urgent things done?

A: It's hard to describe how I manage it. I just do it! For example, I know that I have a phone call on Thursday and I know I should do some prep work for it. But I have bigger deadlines looming today and tomorrow, so I will do the prep work for that call an hour before it starts. I also look for opportunities in my day to fit important, but maybe not urgent, things in. I'm really good at maximizing my hours; in a 40-hour work week, I can often get 40 hours of work done in 30, which means I can spend the other 10 getting a head start on those longer-range things. I also look to maximize my down time. When I watch TV or movies, I'm folding laundry, checking my Blackberry, or something else productive. I'm not really a sit-still person.

reach to be successful: Choose a contractor within two months and start the project before Labor Day. These simple steps ensured that Susan made the phone calls, solicited bids, acquired financing, and finalized decisions on how to complete the backyard improvements before the end of the fall. Without these steps, the project might have dragged on for months. This would not have been because Susan did anything wrong. But without setting goals to complete must-do's that are not urgent, and then creating measurable milestones, our time gets wasted on what is urgent but not critical to our long-term needs.

There are many subjects that people just don't want to talk about, think about, or plan for—death, fires, floods, the list goes on—and yet the probability that at least one of these things will happen at some point is highly likely. Why is it that people who live in a hurricane area rush to stores to buy water and batteries just before a storm hits, often finding that critical items are out of stock? Don't they know that storms come their way each year and that they need these items? Of course they do, but somehow not preparing in advance makes people feel better—that is, until clouds loom on the horizon. Then panic sets in.

Focus is about *preparation*, and that includes preparing for the unexpected. Take a few minutes right now and make a list of what you would need if the following happened:

- You or someone close to you were killed or became seriously ill
- A natural disaster struck in your town
- Your home caught fire

Chances are your list includes any or all of the following items: emergency preparedness kit, fire extinguishers, emergency contact numbers, earthquake kit (with water and nonperishable food items), a will, power of attorney or health care proxy documents. Make a list of those items and incorporate them into your big picture goals. Parents should have wills; people who live in areas likely to be hit with natural disasters should have kits and a plan. Set a goal to get these things done in the next two months. You'll feel great once you do.

Alicia set a great example of being prepared. "We lived in Manhattan after 9/11 and I had an extensive emergency kit. Water, diapers, flashlights, radios . . . I had it all. My husband and some friends thought I was a bit nuts and chocked it up to being a new mom. Why spend the money to do this? Why use precious apartment space to store this stuff? Chances are this was not an event that was going to occur again. Well guess what? About eighteen months later, something did happen. It was thankfully not a terrorist attack but a citywide blackout lasting over twenty-four hours. I was prepared. We had food, water, a radio to get information, and lots of flashlights. After that, my husband, Adam, apologized and even helped me get our earthquake kit together when we move to Los Angeles a few years later."

SCHEDULE "BE YOU" TIME

The one thing that almost never makes it on to-do lists—short or long term—is time to *be you*. We call it "BU" time, and it is critical to your sanity that it makes it on both your lists. This can be as simple as scheduling time to work out or see friends, visiting your doctor and dentist on a regular basis, or planning date nights for you and your spouse. Make yourself a priority! Include something just for you on your weekly to-do list. Write it down, make it a priority, and stick to it. You deserve it!

A Pretty Neat Tip

REMEMBER THE BIG 4

Water, food, cash, and first-aid supplies are the foundation of any emergency kit. Make sure you have enough to last each person in the house at least five days.

CHAPTER WRAP-UP

There aren't enough hours in the day to do everything, so hard choices have to be made. One of the core principles of Buttoned Up is focusing on what *really* matters and eliminating the rest. It sounds easy enough in theory, but it seems to be a universal challenge in reality. Most people do prioritize their lists, but upon closer inspection, deadlines are really driving their action plans. The net result is that things like you, your long-range planning, and other priorities fall by the wayside. Being driven by deadlines is exhausting, frustrating, and essentially like being stuck on a treadmill going too fast to nowhere. Get focused on what really matters by employing at least one (but ideally two or more) of the following techniques:

- *Incorporate Big Picture Planning.* Take time out for yourself at least once every three months to think about your long-range goals. Break them down into smaller steps and incorporate them into your regular to-do lists.
- *Ask Your To-Do List "Why?"* Examine your to-do list every Monday and distinguish which items are truly important versus just make-work. Ruthlessly eliminate the unimportant (but often urgent) make-work.
- *Measure Your Progress.* Assigning metrics to success will keep you honest and on track. Define concrete milestones with due dates and track your progress.
- *Plan for the Unexpected.* Outline what you would need if you or a loved one became incapacitated from an illness or if there was a natural disaster. Use the list to create an emergency plan for yourself and your family. Don't wait until it is too late.

- *Schedule "Be You" Time.* Block off thirty minutes to an hour every other day to recharge your own batteries. Put it in your agenda or in your electronic calendar so that you don't schedule over it.

MANAGE YOUR EMERGENCIES

Why is it that the only time we think to get prepared is when disaster is breathing down our necks? So often we hear about hurricanes, fires, earthquakes, and other disasters and think, "I should really put a few things together in case of an emergency . . . " But we never get around to doing anything about it.

Preparing for the unexpected is less daunting than you might think. Websites abound that can help you develop an action plan. In general, it should take less than three hours to prepare for the unexpected. That's right, isn't your family's safety worth one night of prime-time TV? If that still seems overwhelming, break it into bite-size pieces. Assign one week as emergency preparedness week and have your family spend thirty minutes a night going through the steps of handling an emergency together. Once everyone agrees on what to do, write it down and post it in the house.

ENGAGE THE ENTIRE FAMILY

Getting prepared should not be a burden for one person to carry. For example, if you're building an emergency kit, assign each family member a task—whether it's buying supplies or clearing out space to store the kits—and encourage him or her to get it done within a week.

GET EXTRAS

Stock up on items critical to you and your family that may be difficult to get during an emergency. Examples include prescription medication; glasses and contact lenses, including saline solution; and baby items, such as formula and diapers.

For more tips and information on preparing for unexpected emergencies or disasters, check out the Department of Homeland Security website at www.ready.gov/america/index.html.

---

1. Gallup Poll, "Half of Americans Pressed for Time; a Third Are Stressed Out," May 2004. Survey link: http://www.gallup.com/poll/11545/half-americans-pressed-time-third-stressed.aspx.

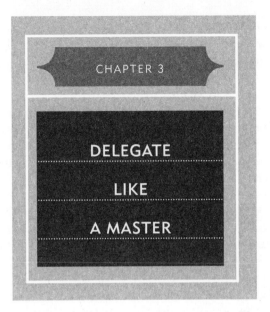

CHAPTER 3

DELEGATE

LIKE

A MASTER

"Never tell people how to do things. Tell them what to do

and they will surprise you with their ingenuity."

—GEORGE S. PATTON

Delegating is tough, particularly when it comes to non-work-related tasks. It's hard to do at all, let alone do well. You're likely to struggle with it whether you work outside the home or not. Those who delegate well did not become masters overnight. It's a hard-won skill cultivated over time. If you've ever said to yourself, "I wish there were more hours in the day," then it's a skill worth developing. Delegation is one of the best tools we know of to help you tackle your to-do list and ensure that there's enough time in your schedule to take care of yourself.

When we talked to people about the barriers to delegation, the notion that "it's easier to just do it myself" kept coming up over and over again. For many, that's simply a knee-jerk response to why they don't employ the power of delegation. Most people are either too busy with their to-do lists to worry about how to add new techniques to their organizational toolbox or unwilling to relinquish control for fear tasks won't be accomplished the way they'd like. Other contributors to delegation denial include ingrained habits and personality traits that prevent us from embracing this valuable skill. Fret not! Anyone can learn to delegate, you just need to find out what kind of delegator you are and find your equilibrium.

IDENTIFY YOUR INNER DELEGATOR

In our travels, we found that people are generally one of three types when it comes to delegating: Control Freaks, Conflicteds, and Zen Masters.

CONTROL FREAKS

Control Freaks, not surprisingly, delegate sparingly, and even then often un-delegate what has been delegated. They want things done the way they want them done—thank you very much—and won't rest until they're done that way. They're also more likely to throw their hands up in frustration when they realize the time required to delegate effectively.

Nina Restieri, self-described Control Freak, admits, "I'm really bad at delegating. Maybe it's because I know if I want it done right, I have to do it myself." Darcy Ahl paddles in the same boat. "At the end of day, if I want it done right, I just do it myself. The hardest thing about it for me is that nobody is as much a perfectionist as I am; nobody cares like I do. So I just do it. I know it's not so constructive; my family calls me Master and Commander!" Dr. Smith agrees: "I delegate what I have to, but I don't do it often enough. Part of it is that I don't trust people to do a good enough job. To do it effectively, you really have to do it yourself."

CONFLICTEDS

Conflicteds, like the name suggests, struggle with both asking for help and letting go. They aren't afraid of entrusting others with a task, but they have a hard time determining an appropriate level of follow-up and communication to ensure that the task is being done to a high enough standard. When things aren't done to their liking, they may retrench, thinking it's faster and easier to do it themselves.

A Pretty Neat Tip

MAKE A DO-NOT-DELEGATE LIST

We found that most people have one or two things that drive them completely crazy if not done their way. For some it's making the beds, for others it's folding the laundry just so. They get a sense of gratification both from doing the work and seeing their desired outcome.

Don't worry! It's okay to have a few tasks you don't want to relinquish to others. Simply determine what you absolutely *cannot* let go of, for whatever reason, and don't delegate those tasks. Think about it: If you can't let it go, you're using more time and energy trying to delegate it than if you just did it yourself.

But there's a catch!

Limit yourself to *no more than two* do-not-delegate tasks. Yes, just two. Otherwise, you will be back to trying to do it all and failing miserably.

How do you do this? Make a list of all of the tasks you delegate (at work and at home) and the tasks you would consider letting someone else do. Pick two items you really don't want to delegate, particularly tasks you can't accept being done any other way but your own. Make sure that keeping them on your to-do list won't derail you from doing more important things. Then give yourself permission to continue doing these tasks by yourself, your way. That being said, we've found that as people get better at delegating, they have an easier time letting go of even these off-limits tasks.

Cherell Jordin, working mom of two, puts it this way. "I do delegate chores and the organization of our physical space to my husband and kids, but I'm not too happy with the results. I can't seem to get the kids to do their stuff well at all. And my husband does an okay job, although I think there's room for improvement." She concludes with the thought, "I need some advice on delegation."

Kim Yorio recognizes that she'd "have to sleep four hours less each night to get it all done perfectly the way I want it . . . and then I'd end up in the hospital!" She delegates but admits she struggles with it. "The biggest challenge, especially for women, is that you feel it is inappropriate to put upon others."

Working mom Amy Grabow acknowledges that even though her husband is a stay-at-home dad, delegating things like buying birthday gifts and scheduling play dates is difficult. "It's harder for me to let go of. I don't love the way he is doing it . . . 'Did he get the right birthday gifts for kids? Did he schedule enough play dates?' But I know if I'm patient, we'll get there."

ZEN MASTERS

The Zen Masters are proficient when it comes to delegating. They have a good sense for what tasks on their lists should be delegated, to whom they should be assigned, and to what standard they should be done. They have a knack for enlisting the help of others in a way that empowers them, helps them grow, and gets the job done well. But even Zen Masters have a tendency to underestimate the amount of time they spend on routine or repetitive tasks, or those that require very little skill.

Rosemary Biagioni considers herself a strong delegator, and for good reason. "I consider myself to be a good delegator because I teach well. I never make it seem like it's the dictator mom or boss directing or demanding. I much prefer to motivate people to do things, not boss them. I try to motivate my kids in that same spirit. Everybody likes to be treated well, and when you keep that in mind, it helps you tone it down."

Kate Hosford admits to becoming a strong delegator out of necessity. "I had to learn to let go because I just had so much on my plate. My husband, Chris, and I have pretty much divided up the chores by what we're both good at. Anything with kids, school, their social lives, and their medical lives is all me. Anything to do with finances, travel, or home improvements is all him."

Another thing that is common to Zen Masters is how they frame the concept of delegation. Lacey Pappas puts it this way: "I simply ask my husband for help with things. For example, if we need to do a certain project and there are things he does better than I do, like electrical or yard work, I ask him take the lead because I know I can't—or shouldn't!" Christina Harvell Brown takes it one step further. "I'm really lucky to have someone like my husband to share the load; it makes it more fun," she says.

Zen Masters realize that delegation isn't about achieving an even split of the chores, rather it's about enabling others to give and contribute meaningfully.

BECOMING A ZEN MASTER—STEP I: LET GO

If you're currently languishing in the Control Freak or Conflicted category, don't despair. Although the ability to delegate appears to be one of those all-or-nothing attributes (you either have it or you don't), it is a skill that can be acquired and mastered.

The ability to delegate successfully takes a certain mind-set, and the first step toward adopting that Zen Master state is letting go. You need to surrender to the fact that you cannot do it all; it is impossible do everything and still have sufficient quality time for you, your family, and your friends. You also need to surrender to the fact that there is more than one way to accomplish something; attachment to a single, "right way" is not only a waste of energy, it can be isolating as well. And finally, you need to surrender to the fact that it does not really matter who does the task, as long as it gets done. The world will not end if your husband packs your children's bags for an upcoming trip.

Of course, letting go is immensely difficult. If it were easy to do, we'd all be Zen Masters at delegating. If you're in the habit of charging ahead with tasks yourself and skipping the delegating, it can be very difficult to stop yourself in the moment and consider the alternative. What you need are techniques that you can use to interrupt old patterns of behavior until delegation becomes part of your natural organizational repertoire. The Zen Masters we found used a variety of techniques to help them interrupt Control Freak tendencies and let go.

KATE'S QUESTIONS

To help with letting go, Kate Hosford recommends asking yourself why. "If you're having a hard time delegating something, try to ask yourself what is making you hold on so tightly. For example, if I were holding on to packing the boys' lunches, even though my husband had the time to do it, I'd stop and think it through. I'd admit to myself that the goal is to get them to eat something vaguely nutritious. My husband, Chris, would agree with that goal for sure. We don't buy any junk food, so the kitchen is stocked with nutritious foods, which means whatever gets packed isn't going to be a nutritional disaster. If that little rational self-talk still didn't assuage my conscience, I'd ask myself what else I might be afraid of. Am I afraid the teacher will say something about the quality of their lunches? Am I afraid that my kids will think less of me because I don't make their lunches? Once my brain runs through those ridiculous scenarios, I can ask myself a final question:

Isn't it more important to be less stressed out yourself than to make a perfect lunch? Amazingly, the answer is always yes."

ANN'S COMPASSION

Ann Smith, a single working mom with children ages seven and five, admits to Control Freak tendencies but keeps them at bay by considering the impact of *not* delegating tasks, especially to her children. "I grew up in a household where my mom really went overboard and did everything for her kids and her guests, and as a child I remember feeling powerless, like I wasn't in control of anything and my contributions wouldn't be good enough for my mom. It wasn't pleasant, so naturally I want my kids to have a sense that they have some power, some control, and the ability to make a meaningful contribution to the household. I make a conscious effort to try to delegate to them whenever possible, not because I don't have enough time or don't want to do something, but because I want them to feel empowered."

Ann's technique of stopping and thinking about the impact her controlling tendencies have on others extends to her guests as well. She says, "When friends used to come over and they wanted to help me with dinner or something, I used to say, 'Oh no, there's nothing you can do, just sit down and make yourself comfortable.' But after considering how not being able to pitch in made me feel when I was a guest, I decided to let go and let them pitch in. And when I'm a guest somewhere, and I know the host or hostess is having a hard time with delegating, I will use an old trick I learned from working at the Gap when I was in high school. They taught you to only ask questions that have to be answered by something other than a 'yes' or a 'no.' So, if I really want to help somebody, I wouldn't say 'Can I bring something,' or 'Can I help you?' I'd say, 'What can I bring?' Or 'What can I do to help?' The person can still say nothing, but there's a little less instant dismissal; it tends to make people think a little bit more. Then you can try to read from them what sounds most appealing and pitch in and do that."

ALISON'S PARAMETERS

Alison Lord is mom to two girls, caretaker of two sick parents, a tireless volunteer, and a force to be reckoned with in the world of advertising. She admits to being a Control Freak when it comes to getting things done the right way. But she also believes in the importance of delegating well, particularly at home. "I think there's an instinct to coddle your kids. But they need to have the skills and the drive to do things like housekeeping chores well. When you live with others, you have an obligation to the people you live with to pull your weight in that sense." To help her let go, she articulated some clear parameters for delegating. "I've figured out what the Control Freak in me is okay delegating, and what it's not. I'm fine with delegating housekeeping-related tasks like emptying the dishwasher, emptying and folding the laundry, cleaning up the clutter, and meal prep, but when it comes to foundational tasks, like organizing a linen closet, I know that nobody else cares enough to do it really thoughtfully (or wants to do it for that matter), so anything requiring a system I will not delegate."

BECOMING A ZEN MASTER—STEP II: ESTABLISH STANDARDS AND STEP BACK

Just because you have relinquished a task does not mean you should give up hope of having it done well. In fact, one of the biggest barriers to delegation is the notion that others won't be able to complete the task to your standards. Effective delegation just doesn't work that way. Everyone has their own unique way of seeing the world and doing things. If you insist on standing over others, telling them how the task must be done, nagging them, and criticizing their approach along the way, not only will they feel frustrated and discouraged, but they will also be much less willing to help you with future tasks. Instead, establish clear standards that provide others with goals for completing the task well. Be specific about what it means to get the job done to these standards, then step back and trust that they will complete it well. As General Patton said, let people surprise you with their ingenuity.

MARCI'S STANDARDS FOR HER CHILDREN'S ROOMS

Marci Miller, who we met earlier, is mom to four kids ages five to thirteen. She has learned to successfully set high standards for her children and then trust them to get the job done. "I have no choice but to delegate. With four kids, there is just too much going on. When it comes to their bedrooms, I've gotten to the point where I don't even have to look at them or inspect them anymore. They know that their beds must be made before they leave the house in the morning and that all the clothes must be put away. As long as they have done those things, it is good enough for me. I don't worry if their rooms look perfect or their beds have been made with hospital corners. The important thing is that when I walk by a room, it meets my standard of cleanliness, and that is all that matters. I had to learn to totally let go in

TAKE THE ULTIMATE DELEGATION QUIZ!

Do you believe that "to get it done right, I have to do it myself"? Have you ever reloaded a fully loaded dishwasher or refolded imperfectly folded laundry? Or at least thought about it? Take this quiz to see how sharp your delegation skills really are.

RATE HOW YOU FEEL ABOUT THE FOLLOWING STATEMENTS:

There is a right way and a wrong way to do everything.
- A. Agree
- B. Neither agree nor disagree
- C. Disagree

If I want it done right, I have to do it myself.
- A. Agree
- B. Neither agree nor disagree
- C. Disagree

How often do you just do something yourself because it is faster and easier in the moment?
- A. Always/Most times
- B. Sometimes
- C. Rarely/Never

Pick the statement that best describes you.
- A. I never have enough time in the day to get it all done; the only time I relax is when I collapse into bed. As soon as I awake, the stress kicks in again.
- B. I manage to get everything important done, but I have to stay up pretty late some nights to do it all.
- C. My life is full, but I have things enough under control that I have time to relax.

order to focus on the more important things I needed to stay on top of, like homework and schedules."

Once you establish clear guidelines for a job well done, it's easy for others to check their own progress against those standards. The first few times you delegate a task to someone, especially a child at home, allow some time to check their work and provide constructive feedback. Only accept it as done when you are satisfied that it meets your standards. If, as a parent, you accept a partly completed or poorly done task, you'll end up investing more time completing it, and your child will miss out on a valuable learning opportunity.

Which would you rather do?
  A. Sleep
  B. Go to yoga
  C. Do the laundry

In reality, which would you most likely do?
  A. Do the laundry
  B. Sleep
  C. Go to yoga

If you answered mostly As, you're what is affectionately known as a Control Freak. You want things done the way you want them done—thank you very much—and you won't rest until they're done that way. You care more than anyone else does about the way something should be done, and you won't stop at being pushy to get your way. Your high standards are certainly a strength, but your inability to relinquish control can make it a challenge to complete all your tasks, let alone secure any downtime.

If you answered mostly Bs, you're a Conflicted—a little conflicted about the concept of delegation. You don't always like asking others for help because you don't want to put them out or appear too demanding. You're certainly capable of entrusting others with a task, yet you struggle with appropriate follow-up and communication to ensure that the task is being done to a high enough standard.

If you answered mostly Cs, you're a Zen Master, a proficient delegator. You have a good sense for what tasks should be delegated, to whom they should be assigned, and to what standard they should be done. You have the knack for enlisting the help of others in a way that empowers them and helps them grow—and in a way that gets the job done. You may underestimate the amount of time you spend on routine or repetitive tasks, or those that require very little skill.

ANGELA'S TRICKS FOR TRUSTING

Michigan lawyer Angela Sujek, mom to two boys, eight and eleven, uses standards to let go of things that are not being done her way. Rather than focus on *how* something is done, she focuses on the end game. "I don't feel that I am the only one who can do it right . . . well, maybe I feel that way a *little* bit! But I obviously think it's worthwhile to have the kids and my husband help out. We all share in the family responsibilities and everyone has something on his to-do list. My husband helps with cooking. He may not do it the way I'd do it, but as long as food is on the table, we're in good shape. The kids do their own laundry. They don't fold exactly the way I want them to, but they put their clothes away, which is the point as far as I am concerned. Every once in a while I will wash and fold their things my way, but in general I just leave it alone. I want my kids to feel good about themselves and their contributions. If they do what is expected of them—for example, make their own beds every day—that is more important than if the sheets are tucked in a certain way. I could do it all myself . . . but I would not get much sleep! Delegation is a hard thing to do. It really depends on your personality. *Your* way is not always the right way and you need to let other people be who they are. There is more than one way to get something accomplished."

BECOMING A ZEN MASTER—STEP III: GIVE FEEDBACK

It is not enough to simply ask someone to do something, then articulate standards and give them room to complete the task. How you react to their finished product has a huge impact on their willingness to take on future tasks. Think about what motivates a person to get something done and use that when giving feedback. For example, if you know somebody responds well to praise, and they've done a good job on a project, give them positive feedback for sure, but also praise them in front of others for their incredible job. Be specific about what they have done well.

● PRETTY NEAT WISDOM ●

TRY IT! YOU'LL LIKE IT

Learning to delegate effectively is as simple as giving it a try! Ask the people in your life for a little help. Start with simple things, like the dishes or a small task at the office, and then go from there. Remember, to be successful you must do the following:

• Relinquish control
• Motivate the person to whom you delegate
• Understand and embrace the trade-offs of delegating tasks

The more you practice, the better you will get. And the more you delegate, the more time you'll have to focus on what really matters in your life.

Gina Bernstein, mom to three, might have said it best: "When you delegate, you cannot be critical of others. If you ask someone to do something, you have to accept that they may not necessarily do it the way you would have done it, and that is just fine."

NANCY'S CARROT

For Nancy Meyer, getting her college-age daughter, Marissa, to clean up her room is all about using carrots. "Marissa's room is often a mess, with clothes on the floor and on the bed. It doesn't bother me, really. I usually just close her door, but when I *do* want her to clean it up, it is all about what I will give her if she does it. It doesn't have to be a lot, but sometimes just the promise of an inexpensive pair of shoes is all it takes for that room to be completely transformed. It's worth it to me and to her, and it saves us from fighting about it."

Should you offer incentives and rewards for a job well done? Will praise or threats be more effective? What really works to motivate others to complete tasks to your standards? The short answer is that it depends on the person and the task. Here are a few common carrots and sticks to consider using as reward or punishment for completing tasks.

Carrots
- Allowance (or any form of financial reward)
- Privileges (staying up late, watching a favorite TV show)
- Praise
- Release from another chore
- Doing something for that person in return

Sticks
- Withholding allowance
- Losing privileges
- Poor evaluation (or review, if work related)
- Being grounded
- Not delivering on a promise or reward

No matter what type of feedback you choose to give, your job as a delegator is not complete until you have given it.

FOCUS ON THE TRADE-OFFS

When delegating a task to someone else and agreeing to let go of the results, it's important to know what you're gaining in return. This often motivates people to get over the hump and into the groove of making delegation part of their daily routine.

Business experts know that if you want X product made or X job done, it can be accomplished several ways, all of which come with inherent costs

Meet: Frederick Hawkins (with some input from his wife, Manuela)

Family: Married with one son

Occupation: Frederick is a brand strategist and founder of NewYork-DadBlog.com; Manuela is cofounder of EcoBabyBuys.com.

Q: When it comes to delegating, would you consider yourselves to be Control Freaks, Conflicteds, or Zen Masters?

A: Well, we both have our "things," but on the whole Manuela is a little bit more relaxed than I am. I'm a neat freak in the OCD sense of the word, so I wouldn't say I'm a Zen Master. I really care about how things are placed in a room; I have strong opinions about how things should look. So I pretty much never delegate room clean up (yes, I probably would "redo" something that had been done already just because it wasn't done "right"). With that said, having a child has really helped me let go of those OCD tendencies. It's about survival! Stressing yourself about the way toy clutter looks isn't going to change anything, and at a certain point it isn't worth the energy. I'm learning to pick and choose my battles. Sometimes it's okay if the Lego's stay out.

Q: What are you good at delegating?

A: As much of a neat freak as I am, there's something about laundry that I just can't handle. So I am really good at letting go of that. I'll lug the bag downstairs to our apartment building's laundry room and back up again, but the rest I delegate to Manuela. She, on the other hand, hates doing the dishes, and that's my strong

of time, money, or quality. This same principle applies to delegation. Think about it. You delegate the laundry to your teenager. You gain time and money (e.g., you don't have to potentially pay a housekeeper to do it) but you probably have to give up a little bit on quality (where quality means getting it washed and folded your way). Or, if a task is work-related, you might hire a consultant to complete it. You gain time and quality but you give up money. If you do the task yourself, you most likely get quality and save or earn money, but you sacrifice time.

Write down the top ten tasks you currently want to delegate. Next to each task, write the two things you'll gain by delegating the task and the one thing you will sacrifice. Remember, the choices are time, quality, and money. Go down the list and see what really matters to you in terms of the trade-off.

point. So she delegates that to me. You know, we never really sat down and divided up a list formally, but we have ended up in a place where we have each taken on the chores that suit our strengths. I never worry about the things on her list and she doesn't worry about the things on my list. We both know the other person is going to do a much better job of what's on their list than we would ourselves.

Q: What has helped you let go of things you used to need to do yourself?

A: Well, we both want to be able to do things that *aren't* chores once our son is asleep. If we didn't figure out how to divide and conquer, we'd never have any down time. Plus, kids just force you to adjust your standards a bit. For example, when our son was smaller, I'd wipe his face every two seconds when he was eating. But after awhile, Manuela would just shoot me one of those "chill out" glances and pretty soon I caught on to the fact that he's just going to be a mess when he eats. Full stop. Trying to keep him perfectly neat during meal times just made me (and everyone else) nuts. Now I just back off and let Manuela feed him without swooping in. We all have a lot more fun.

Q: Are you able to hold others to your standards when you delegate? What's your secret?

A: Well, we both had neat-freak moms. So it is hard! It's in our DNA. I think I have a harder time letting go of my perfectionist standards than Manuela does, much to her chagrin. But having our son has been a transformative experience. I just try to ask myself if a task is worth it—and more importantly—by obsessing over whatever it is, am I disrupting our son's routine? Any time we go around those routines for any reason, things, well, they just don't go as smoothly as they should.

You will often find that the two tasks you're least likely to delegate are the ones where the outcome or quality matter to you most. The rest are items where the benefits outweigh the costs.

CHAPTER WRAP-UP

Although the ability to delegate appears to be one of those all or nothing things (you either have it or you don't), it is a skill that can be acquired and mastered. Below are the three steps to effective delegation.

- *Step I—Let Go:* Letting go is immensely difficult. Ask yourself, "What am I afraid of?" Consider the impact *not* delegating has on the people you love. Make delegation part of your natural organizational repertoire.

- *Step II—Establish Standards and Step Back:* When you delegate tasks, you give up control of exactly how the job will be done, but not of having it done to your standards. Set standards by being specific about how and when tasks should be completed.
- *Step III—Provide Feedback:* When delegating tasks to people, it's not enough to simply articulate standards and give them room to complete the job. How you react to their finished product affects their willingness to take on future tasks. Think about ways to motivate others and use that when giving feedback.

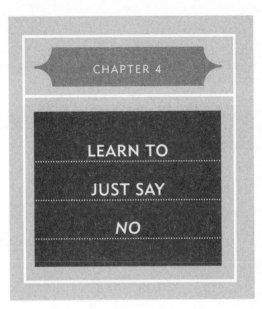

CHAPTER 4

LEARN TO

JUST SAY

NO

"Half of the troubles of this life can be traced to saying

yes too quickly and not saying no soon enough."

—JOSH BILLINGS

Why can't we just spit it out? *No.* N. O. These are two letters any two-year-old and most sixty-year-olds can string together with ease and a fair amount of boldness. But something happens to us between our toddler years and our golden years. By the time people reach their early teens or twenties, most will have either completely lost the ability to string together those two simple letters, or at least find it incredibly difficult to spit them out without a whole lot of equivocating. Only after a few decades of hard work, chronic overextension, and stress do we slowly regain the ability to say no.

Irina Baranov, thirty-eight-year-old wife, mother of two, daughter, sister, friend, and marketing director for the nonprofit Council for Relationships in Philadelphia, sums up the dilemma elegantly. "It's only after we've suffered the consequences of too many *yes's* that the word *no* loses its edge and can become a complete sentence again." She continues, "I have a friend who joked that the way you say no in your twenties is 'Yes, and what else can I do for you?' And that's so true! Relearning how to say no takes practice. It takes years to get it right."

WHY DO WE SAY *YES* WHEN WE REALLY MEAN *NO*?

Saying no is vital to achieving a Buttoned Up life. Without *no,* finding your focus is an impossibility. Without *no* the quality of your relationships and your work diminishes. Without *no* your time is not your own. Without *no* you lose control. Far from being a negative or bad word, *no* is essential to a sane existence.

So what is it about the word *no* that makes it so difficult to utter? We found that five things tend to suppress our ability to say no: (1) the potent positive feedback you receive when you do something you're naturally good at, (2) an innate desire to be liked, (3) cultural norms, (4) fear of having to justify or fight for your *no,* and (4) your own lack of clarity. Most often, these drivers lie beneath our conscious awareness. We believe they *all* can be overcome. In fact, the many people we spoke to who had reclaimed their ability to say no bear witness to that. But if you're one of the millions still struggling with the concept, perhaps shining a light on these drivers will help you to recognize the dynamics at work in your subconscious so that you can take proactive steps to overcome them, or even better, replace them with more positive, *no* affirming ones.

POTENT POSITIVE FEEDBACK LOOP

From your earliest years, you are conditioned to say yes. When you listen and do what you're told, you are praised and receive lots of positive reinforcement from your parents. When you start school, teachers reward you for doing what they ask you to do. When you begin to form friendships with others, you get positive reinforcement from them by doing things with and for them that make them happy. The same holds true when you begin dating, when you start working, and so on.

Stop and think for a moment about the cumulative effect of all that positive reinforcement around being agreeable. It is potentially staggering, particularly if you are asked to do something that you're naturally good at. Lori Wilson, journalist and co-host of Philadelphia's NBC *The 10! Show*, is frequently asked to make pro bono public appearances because of her naturally effervescent personality. Lori makes every effort to squeeze as many of them as she can into a very busy schedule, in part because of the benefit she receives from positive reinforcement. "I am really bad at saying no, especially if an organization asks specifically for me," she admits. "They tend to be really good causes, and I do want to serve my community, so I go out of my way to accommodate them. I get an amazing amount of positive reinforcement from doing them. I get a feeling I can't really describe; people are so glad and so grateful. In those moments, I think that, if I weren't on TV every day, I'd be a professional host."

Alison Lord, an advertising executive with two daughters, a full social life, and an equally busy husband, just added taking care of ailing parents to her already full schedule. If anyone is in a position to say no to a request, it's Alison. Yet earlier this spring, an old high school classmate called her and asked if she'd help organize their upcoming reunion. "I said, 'I really cannot help. My parents are sick and I've just got too much going on.'" But somehow she ended up coordinating the event anyway. She jokes, "This is me not doing the event: I find a place for the party, I organize a menu, I send the invites. . . ." She admits, "I'm gifted at juggling a lot of things and doing them all well. I like to make connections where there haven't been connections before. And in the end, I'm happy that the event went well; people had a good time. I get a lot of positive reinforcement for doing things well, which obviously feeds on itself."

INNATE DESIRE TO BE LIKED

We all share an innate human desire to be liked. We have been consistently rewarded with parental approval, friendship, good grades, and promotions for towing the line. It's no wonder saying no triggers feelings of guilt—you've been trained that it's wrong! Come to think of it, it's a miracle we ever recover the ability to say no. To some extent, we are programmed to think that saying no or asserting our own needs over others means we've failed in some regard. We're letting someone down.

Ann Smith, a linguist and thirtysomething divorced mom to two, admits, "I have a really hard time saying no. Say I have a friend who asks me to give a talk. Even if I feel sick to my stomach because I know I will have to turn my life upside down to fit it in, I will usually give in. There are lots of things

I do because I think I would be really disappointing the other person if I say no."

Zeyna Ballee, a thirty-year-old working mother of one, adds, "I'd much rather say—and hear—the words 'let me think about it' than an outright no. It means you're acknowledging that what you think they're endeavoring is worthwhile."

CULTURAL NORMS

Like it or not, saying no may not feel as safe for women as it does for men. When you say no, you assert your own agenda, which can be a double-edged sword. Do it too often, or with too much force, and you might be deemed a shrew or selfish.

Kate Hosford, children's author and mother of two, observes, "A lot of women I know don't feel entitled to say no. It's almost as though you have to have something else you're doing in order to say no . . . and it had better be earth-shatteringly important to pass muster." Irina Baranov acknowledges that "girls are still conditioned from an early age to be sweet, to be nice, and to think about making others around them happy. I work in the psychological arena, so I am aware of the issue and I consider myself to be a feminist . . . and yet, I know I instinctively told my daughter exponentially more times to be sweet, to focus on pleasing others, than I told my son. I hate to admit it, but there is definitely a gender piece to the 'no' equation."

When you add in additional complexities like the glass ceiling or just the standard stereotype of women as nurturers, deviating from the expected *yes* can seem risky.

FEAR OF FIGHTING

Assertion of your own desires is made even more difficult when the other person isn't prepared to accept your refusal and you have to defend and "fight" for your no. It can be unpleasant, unnerving, and even scary to have to stick up for yourself. It can be even harder if the person goes on the attack, pushing back on your *no* by putting you down, attacking you, exposing your vulnerabilities, or simply claiming that you are behaving out of character and not like "yourself."

For Ann Smith, the notion of having to justify and fight for her *no* is particularly difficult. "I am already not strong enough in my *no*'s. So when I feel people can or will try to convince me even though I don't want to be convinced otherwise, I feel backed into a corner. If I am wavering internally at all about something, I crumble easily, and then I get angry at myself for being such a wimp."

LACK OF CLARITY

If you say no and the other person counters with "why not?" are you really clear on the answer yourself? Sometimes we're unsure of our own position on something. Maybe you're unsure because you really *do* want to be able to do what's been asked of you but worry you don't have the time or energy. Maybe you're unsure because you don't know if you can do a good enough job. Maybe you're unsure because you aren't clear on the amount of effort required to get the job done. Whatever the ultimate reason for your indecision, in our need-it-now world it can seem unsportsmanlike to beg for more time to consider the request.

SAYING *NO* IN DIFFERENT DECADES

In addition to these five roadblocks to no, you face unique challenges during your twenties and your thirties in particular, which can make saying no even more difficult.

YOUR TWENTIES: SOLIDIFYING YOUR OWN IDENTITY AND STRIVING TO ACHIEVE

Your twenties are all about becoming a truly independent adult. In your early twenties, you become self-supporting (if you aren't already). You identify and begin a plausible career and possibly even select a spouse. By your mid to late twenties, if you're happy with the career you originally selected, you're striving to move up the ladder. If the first career you chose wasn't a good fit, you're identifying a more appropriate alternative. You're nurturing friendships with others who are also coming into their own. It's a period of tremendous growth, but also vulnerability.

You are more sure of who you are than you were in your teens, but fear of rejection still runs high, and there's nothing like a little fear of rejection to stifle a healthy *no*. Fear of your boss's reaction makes you swallow your *no* when she hands you an assignment that you don't have the bandwidth for, unless you burn the midnight oil. Fear of disappointing a friend makes you say yes to an expensive group dinner, even though you're scraping the bottom of your financial barrel. Fear of your parents' disapproval keeps you from ditching a safe, well-paying job even though you hate it. Fear of looking like goody-two-shoes impels you to down that shot the hottie you're on a first date with dares you to drink, even though you know it will impede your ability to make your 6:30 AM yoga class, which you really love. In your twenties, assertion of your individual priorities feels dangerous because it could lead to ostracism by peers, parents, or bosses.

YOUR THIRTIES: LEARNING TO BE RESPONSIBLE FOR OTHERS

The thirties are a crucible. It's a period marked by increased levels of responsibility, like buying your first home, having children, or being given your first really important title at work. Caring for others who are utterly dependent on you for everything is a challenge. So is learning to effectively handle a growing number of obligations simultaneously. Sleep deprivation and stress are hallmarks of the thirties, both of which are exacerbated by the inability to say no to things.

Why is it difficult to say no in your thirties? You generally know who you are and tend to be sure of your own priorities, but knowing how to balance your personal priorities with those of others who are dependent on you can be disorienting and confusing. Are you a bad parent if you decline to chair a committee for your child's school fundraiser? Will you stunt your child's growth if you tell them they cannot participate in an extracurricular activity with a particularly tough travel schedule? Are you failing your spouse if you have to go on an important business trip on his or her birthday? Will you be passed over for a promotion at work in the short-term and possibly the long-term if you turn down that big project that will keep you burning the midnight oil during the first few weeks of your child's life? In your thirties, assertion of your individual priorities feels dangerous because it could be detrimental to someone or something for which you are responsible.

YOUR FORTIES TO FIFTIES: COMING INTO YOUR OWN

By the time you reach your forties and fifties, you've probably experienced enough downsides to saying yes that you're chastened. Although you will face new pressures in these decades, such as caring for aging parents, saying no to things you know will take up your limited bandwidth is much less daunting.

Kathy Ferguson, a fortysomething mother of four who has a huge extended family, exemplifies the reclaimed no. "I used to say yes to everything. I feel like I used to have a big *SAP* sign stuck on my forehead. People would always say, 'Oh, just ask Kathy because she'll do it.' I've reached a point where for every *yes* there has to be a *no* because I need to have enough patience for my kids. I find when I overextend myself with volunteer work, I start to get really impatient with my kids. When I realized that a few years ago, I made a conscious effort to back away from a lot of the stuff I used to do."

Jami Osiecki, a TV producer also in her thirties, says, "I've gotten much better at saying no as I've gotten older. I used to over obligate myself all the time. But I've come to realize that my time is valuable. If I'm going doing something with only half a desire to do it, it's not worth it. Not only do I end up resenting the time I'm putting in, but I'm sure I'm not doing that great of a job at whatever it is that I've been asked to do. Basically, I've organized the people in my life according to tiers. For my immediate family and close friends, the word *no* does not exist. I reserve most of "me" for myself and my inner circle. And now I am quite comfortable organizing/prioritizing my time along those lines."

Janice Raab, working mom of five grown children, used to really struggle with saying no to extended family, but turning fifty has made it much easier. "Hitting fifty means I look at life differently. I mean who knows how long I have left here? There's just not enough time to worry about what others want from me—I'd much rather do what I want to do! Besides, I have lived the downside of not saying no enough times, whether that's hosting big extended family gatherings where I make myself crazy doing everything and miss out on the chance to spend quality time with my kids, or doing something for my mom who is never happy with the output (and often has someone else doing the same thing for her just in case I do it 'wrong'). Now I'm really clear. I just want to enjoy my own kids. I don't need to make excuses or take on something that will get in the way of that."

UNLEASHING YOUR INNER TWO-YEAR-OLD

Saying no at one time or another is difficult for all of us. Take the following scenario: You are invited to your nephew's fifth-grade graduation. It's a big deal to him because it's the end of elementary school; next year, he'll be in middle school. If you say yes and attend, you'll miss an important meeting, have to endure a three-hour drive, and won't make your afternoon workout. In your heart of hearts, you don't really want to go. You don't feel that it's important for you to be there, but you feel guilty saying you can't make it. You're afraid your sister will be upset with you or your mother will call and yell at you. What can you do? After all, you *are* a grown woman. Why can't you just say no and let that be enough?

Saying no gracefully is just not that easy. But it is possible. Many of the women we have spoken to have some very smart, easy-to-use techniques that make saying no easier and give them more control over the outcome.

PUT POLICIES OR RULES INTO EFFECT

It's not unusual to be bombarded with the same kind of request, like volunteering at your child's school, time and time again. Instituting rules or guidelines can make it much easier to say no. Just ask Cindi Leive, editor of *Glamour* magazine. She regularly gets requests from friends and acquaintances to read and review their books in the hopes that she will put a blurb about the book in the magazine. She says, "I used to spend a lot of time reading the books by people I knew. But I eventually learned it was best to make a company-wide policy to deal with the issue. Now we have a policy that we don't do book blurbs at *Glamour*. Obviously, the reason for the policy is because of the ethical issues it presents. But it also makes it easy for me to say no to the constant stream of requests from people asking me to read or review their book. It's not personal, it's just company policy."

Policies don't just apply to the world of work. Nina Restieri, founder of momAgenda and mother to four, has a rule in place for the amount of volunteer work she allows herself to sign up for at her children's school. "I allow myself to do *one* big thing in support of the school for the year. Once I've decided on what that one big thing is, the rule makes it really easy to say no to every other request that comes along. I can simply say, 'I'm doing this one big thing and that's all I can take on this year.' It's so important to realize your limits. I've had situations in the past where I've taken on so much that I found it made me a really bad mother because I'd get so cranky. Having this one simple rule in place has changed everything; it's better for everybody."

BEG FOR TIME AND ASK YOURSELF QUESTIONS

If you really have a difficult time saying no, or find that you're chronically overextended, buying yourself some time to respond is an excellent tactic. Swap your "Sure, no problem" for "That sounds really interesting; let me think about it and get back to you with an answer." If you feel the need to follow up with an additional nicety, try "When do you need a response?" Then use the time to determine whether or not you truly want to accept the request.

This approach has really helped Cynthia Manzo, a San Francisco mom to two toddlers who often struggles with saying no, particularly to requests from her children's caregivers. "When someone who worked for me wanted extra time off with pay or more vacation or something else that I did not necessarily feel was fair, I would automatically say yes because this person was in a way part of the family and I didn't want to upset them. At some point I realized that I felt resentful and taken advantage of. Rather than continue to seethe, I asked my friends what they would do. They reassured me that they would have said no, which is what I wanted to do originally. Then they suggested I buy some time to consider requests, especially ones that I instinctively didn't think were fair. It gives you the ability to consider a request based on its merits, whether it's a request for more paid time off or for volunteering. This technique has given me the ability to say no much more easily, and it hasn't harmed my relationships at all."

The next time you're asked to do something you're not sure you want to do, buy yourself some time before answering. Then ask yourself the following questions, which are designed to help you clarify what *you* really want to do.

1. Why is this person asking me to do this? Is it because she knows I will say yes? Does he rely on me? Have I said yes before?
2. What is my relationship with this person? Is she my close friend? An acquaintance? A relative?
3. Do we have a reciprocal relationship? Am I able to ask her to do the same thing for me and know that she will say yes?
4. Do I feel guilty about saying no? If so, why? For example, do I feel like because I have more time, more money, fewer kids, don't work, etc., I need to say yes to balance things out?
5. Am I wholly responsible for the outcome? If I say no to my friend who wants me to babysit, does she have someone else she can count on? If I don't go to a friend's birthday party, will there be other people there to help her celebrate?
6. What am I giving up if I say yes to this and how does that make me feel?

Once you have answered these questions, you should have more insight about why you want to say no and why you feel uncomfortable saying no to this person or situation. Accepting your reasoning and understanding that it's still okay to decline a request is a critical first step toward saying no.

SCRIPT SOME NO RESPONSES

Sometimes it's easier to have a canned response than to figure out how to respond appropriately in the moment. Since every person is unique and every situation is different, it makes sense to have a few different scripts at the ready.

Take Irina Baranov's friend, Sally. After suffering through decades of saying yes too often, Sally developed a script for saying no that she felt comfortable trotting out when she really needed it. She thought a lot about how to phrase her *no*'s in a way that were firm (no equivocating!) yet considerate. She wanted a soft way to say no that would work well in most situations and came up with a single sentence that did just that: "No, I'm sorry, that doesn't work for me right now."

She says, "I start with the *no*, so it's clear that I cannot do what they're asking. Then I follow with the words *I'm sorry* because when the shoe is on the other foot it's not always easy to hear such a strong *no* right away. I chose the word *that* to describe what's been asked of me because it's a neutral thing. It's not personal at all. I chose the phrase *doesn't work for me* because it reinforces the no in a way that is neither apologetic nor abrasive. And I end with the words *right now* because that leaves open the possibility that if you come back to me at a later time I might be able to help. I also like that the whole script ends on a softer note."

FIND A POINT OF COMPROMISE

Sometimes the best way to deliver a *no* is to suggest an alternative. This is the first thing that Stephanie Wang, a business development manager at an Internet start-up, likes to do. "When I know I can't meet the request being made of me, the first thing I look for is a trade-off. Can I offer something else or suggest an alternative due date to what's been thrown out there that will make both me and the other person happy? If so, I'll immediately suggest that alternative—it's a classic win-win situation. For example, if a friend wants me to meet and screen her new beau but wants me to meet them at a time that conflicts with my favorite spin class, I'll suggest an alternative time that is more convenient for me and might work for her. If that works, everyone is happy. If it doesn't, at least she has had a moment to think about how her request impacts me. At work, if I'm asked to help out on a project that I know I don't have time to manage on my own but would still like to be involved in, I suggest doing it with another person on the team. If there's nobody else who can help, I will ask my boss which project he'd prefer I focus my energy on. That way he understands implicitly that I can't do everything really well and he needs to tell me what the priority is. I love it when I can do what's asked of me without having to turn my life upside down in the process, and this technique really helps me do that."

CHAPTER WRAP-UP

Saying no is vital to achieving a Buttoned Up life. Far from being a negative or bad word, the word *no* is essential to a sane existence. There are many reasons saying no is difficult. We're programmed from an early age to do what we're told, we get lots of positive reinforcement when we say yes, we don't want to hurt anyone's feelings, etc. If you're suffering the consequences of too many yes's and not enough no's, here are some effective techniques for saying it gracefully.

- *Establish Policies*—If you are frequently asked to do something, instituting rules or guidelines can make it easier to say no. This technique is effective for work-related requests, like contributing to a group gift at work, and personal requests, like volunteering at school.
- *Beg for Time and Ask Yourself Questions*—Swap your "Sure, no problem" for "That sounds really interesting; let me think about it and get back to you with an answer." Then use the time to determine whether or not you want to accept the request.
- *Script Some "No" Responses*—Sometimes it's easier to have a canned response than to figure out how to respond appropriately in the moment. Since every person is unique and every situation different, it makes sense to have a few different scripts at the ready.
- *Find a Point of Compromise*—Sometimes the best way to deliver a no is to suggest an alternative. Try offering to do something else or suggest an alternative due date that will make both you and the other person happy.

A Pretty Neat Tip

GET IN THAT DRIVER'S SEAT!

If saying no is something that makes you uncomfortable, try practicing! Stand in front of a mirror and bring on those no's. Imagine what you'd like to say to the person and consider what their response might be. How you would respond? Taking the time to rehearse a conversation will make you less anxious and much better prepared for the real thing. You'll know what to say, especially if the person tries to convince you to say yes.

If you're lucky enough to have bought yourself some time, how will you deliver your answer? You may not always have control over how and when you have the discussion, but when you do, think about the best channel for communicating your message: In person? On the phone? Via email? There's no right answer, but we've found that when you anticipate significant pushback or you're not close to the person who made the request, phone and email are the easiest to use. Saying no is not easy, so do what is easiest and least stressful for you.

Meet: Cindi Leive

Family: Married with two children

Occupation: Editor of *Glamour* magazine

Q: Do you have a hard time saying no?

A: It can be really difficult to force yourself to say no to outside obligations that pop up along the way. Everybody's got something for me to do, see, and look at. I really like to accommodate people, and serving on boards and agreeing to do things like informational interviews for friends' children have merit and really do turn out to be fun. But if I'm not careful, I end up spending so much time doing things for other people that I don't have time to focus on the things that are truly important to me. So I've gradually learned to say no to things without too much guilt.

Q: How do you say no to personal requests that come up?

A: If I really truly don't have enough time, I won't agree to do something. Ironically, the economy has given cover to a lot of people—including me. It's much easier now to say, "We're so buttoned down at work, I'm just not able to participate in XYZ." I've also learned to be very explicit, to really ask how much time something is going to take. Even though it's very difficult, I always ask. For example, if someone wants me to serve on a volunteer board, I'll ask them to walk me through how many meetings they want me to attend over the course of a year, along with any expectations they have of me beyond that. I try to lead into that conversation gracefully, by saying something like, "You have such an incredible organization, I wouldn't want to say yes if I couldn't give 100 percent, so let's talk through the details." The more explicit you can be upfront, the happier all parties will be at the end of the day.

Q: Are you able to say no professionally? If so, how do you do it gracefully?

A: I guess the situation that comes up the most involves staff interaction. I tend to have an open door policy at work and people are used to coming in and having their questions answered fairly immediately. I really like being in the daily flow, so in general that open door works really well for me. But there are times when I need to focus intently on something. In those moments, I have to say to people coming into my office, "I'm sorry, I can't talk about this today." Sometimes I have to close my door to shut out intrusions. When that happens, I try to do it in a way that shows the other person what I have on my plate. I share the reasons I can't do it so people don't feel it's about them. Typically, I say "I can't right now—I'm working on a deadline myself," which makes the *no* much more comfortable.

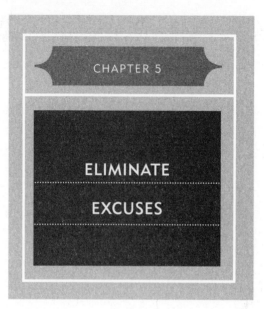

CHAPTER 5

ELIMINATE

EXCUSES

"I attribute my success to this—I never gave or took any excuse."

—FLORENCE NIGHTINGALE

In his hip-hop anthem "Baby Got Back," Sir Mix-A-Lot professes, "I like big butts and I cannot lie." His preference for a round derriere gave him a number one hit and even won him a Grammy back in 1993. Well, we have it on pretty good authority that when he carefully crafted his lyrics, he wasn't referring to those "buts" that keep many of us from getting organized.

That's where we come in. We need to talk about a different kind of "but"—the one gracing the end of the statement: "I really want to get that organized, but . . ." It's big all right, but not in a good way. It's an excuse, and it's keeping you from being as organized as you want or need to be. It's time to find out why. We know that you want to (you did pick up this book after all) and we know that you're trying. In fact, the whole country is trying. In

2008, Americans spent more than $7 billion on storage and organization products.[1] Yet the majority of people we polled still say they are falling short of the mark.

So what's standing in our way? A little procrastination is certainly normal, but ... those darn buts quickly turn a little normal procrastination into permanent avoidance. As it turns out, when we make an excuse and repeat it often enough, it becomes a belief. The belief then becomes a self-fulfilling prophecy. Take, for example, Hollie Sehrt, a graphic designer in her midtwenties. Her "but" to organizing her computer files is that she believes it's a bigger job than it really is. She explains, "I just think it will take too long, at least a few hours, and I don't believe I will ever have enough time set aside to complete such a time-intensive, noncritical task. It's also something that I've convinced myself I could only do well all at once, rather than completing the task in separate chunks. If I'm really honest with myself, that's probably not true, but it reinforces my decision to keep putting off the task."

Excuses are like stop signs; they halt your progress and become a temporary remedy to your problem. Only when you eliminate the excuse and take responsibility for the task can you find solutions to your organizational buts.

HOW BIG IS YOUR ORGANIZATIONAL *BUT*?

There are a million reasons we make excuses when it comes to getting organized, but the fact of the matter is, most will fall into one of four categories.

PERCEPTION VS. REALITY

We all have times when our perception, the way we see things, may not match the reality of the situation. Sometimes we think a task will be more difficult than it really is, and this seems especially true when it comes to organization. Think about it: How many times have you glanced at a project on your to-do list or at a messy pile of papers or at your jumbled closet and decided that tackling it was simply going to be too time-consuming, expensive, or complicated to handle right now? You feel justified putting it off, right? I mean, why bother getting started if you don't have the time, money, or skill to tackle something. As long as your perception is that the task is more than you can handle, it will remain undone.

Julie Waltzer, 28-year-old corporate event planner and married mom-to-be, had one such task lingering for over two years. "Three years ago, my husband and I moved into a new house. We loved everything about the big, oversized master bedroom except for the sliding-door closet. With zero hanging space it was the least user-friendly space in the house, and we let it become a huge mess. I convinced myself that it would be expensive to have a new closet system installed, and the thought of taking all those clothes out was not appealing. Finally we got fed up and called one of those closet companies, and the designer basically told us we didn't need to do much—just take out some shelves and hang an extra bar to make the space usable. We did it ourselves, and fixing our disastrous closet ended up costing about $25 and five hours of our time. I'm still in shock. In my head, the closet was such a huge problem that I put it off, and we lived with it for three years longer than we had to."

Julie learned the hard way that perception does not always match reality. The same holds true for you. It's time to take a second look at anything lingering behind a "but . . ." on your organizational wish list. You may discover that, in reality, the task is perfectly manageable after all.

PERFECTIONISM

Another thing that leads to big organizational buts is perfectionism. Perfectionists tend to get stuck because they have such clear, and, well, perfect standards. If you think something has to get done perfectly, and you know your chances of achieving perfection are limited because you don't have enough time, the right ingredients, or something along those lines, why start?

Sarah Smith, a management consultant with two children, has a perfectionist's block when it comes to getting organized to cook. She explains, "My mom, who worked full time and raised three children, was an absolutely stellar cook; one of those women who can whip up a three-star, four-course meal when the only ingredients in the house are a can of beans and an old lemon. She can bake like Martha Stewart, too. I, on the other hand, am not so creative in the kitchen. I need recipes, and even when I follow them, my creations never seem to turn out like the pictures or taste as good as my mom's cooking. I know that eating in would save our family hundreds of dollars a year and do wonders for my waistline. I also know I'd enjoy the actual cooking, too, because when I do take the time to put together a nice meal, I always feel great. But I just can't seem to get over the hump of planning to do it and making it into a routine. I've tried once or twice to plan out a weekly menu, shop for the menu, and cook all week. But I get so intimidated by the fact that I know my creation won't be nearly as good as the picture suggests, or what I remember my mom's dish tasted like, that I psych myself out. Instead I end up buying a lot of quick pasta meals and ordering takeout. I clearly need to figure out how to overcome my cooking block, which probably comes down to adjusting my expectations of the end result."

Jackie Simon, a clerk for a federal judge, also struggles with perfectionist tendencies that stop her in her tracks. "I've been known to buy new clothes rather than tackle the massive laundry pile because when I do laundry, it must be done perfectly. I need to have special conditioning soap for delicates, the right fabric softener for the dryer, and then time to fold the clothes perfectly. I find myself putting off other chores, too, like cleaning my bathroom, because of my need to do things perfectly. Honestly, my bathroom is the tiniest space, but it takes me two hours to clean it—I literally have to empty the shower of everything so I can scrub every little corner. When it comes to dinner, my boyfriend can whip something up in five minutes. Not me. And honestly? The fact that he can do it so quickly deters me from ever making dinner. If I don't have a good three hours, then dinner is going to be takeout. I have to do things right, which means that on most days when I don't have the time to do something right, I'm just not going to do it."

PRETTY NEAT WISDOM

BIGGER BUTS AREN'T BETTER

Bigger isn't better when it comes to organizational buts. The cumulative effect of too many excuses, and thus too much "white noise," from disorganized things in your life is negative. When you postpone tasks, you continue to carry those unfinished to-do's, which saps you of energy, diminishes your confidence, and keeps you treading water instead of moving forward. Perhaps worst of all, procrastination renders relatively simple tasks very difficult. Postpone anything long enough and it will take on epic proportions, dooming you to spend more time and energy than is necessary wrangling it into completion.

FEAR

Confronting your own mortality, facing how little you really save each month, or thinking about the prospect of being robbed can be intimidating, even downright scary. To get things like wills, life insurance, long-term financial plans, and property insurance squared away, you have to face these fears head-on. When you're afraid of something that might happen in the future, the natural human tendency is to look for ways to escape or avoid dealing with the issue at hand. The problem is that avoidance and escape still leave you vulnerable.

Susan Lerner, divorced mom to four grown children, learned too late about the importance of confronting her fears about the financial details of her life. "After thirty-seven years of marriage, my husband abruptly walked out on me to be with another woman. It came as a total shock. My role had always been to be the caregiver, the nurturer, so I knew everything there was to know about the kids, their birthdays, their hopes, and dreams . . . but I was totally in the dark when it came to our joint finances. I am not particularly good at math and, in all honesty, thinking about things like death, illness, or even divorce, really make me uncomfortable. So I avoided thinking about our finances. Over the years, I happily handed off all responsibility for managing our finances to my ex-husband and never pushed to have him sit down with me and explain the big picture. Unfortunately, when he left it meant I was in an extremely vulnerable position. It was a nightmare trying to gather the information after the fact."

Susie Feldstein, a certified public accountant with three children, saw her mother go through something similar—not once, but twice. "My mom avoided taking ownership of the family finances. When we were younger, she got burned from my dad in a divorce. Happily, she found love again and married my stepdad, who was a wonderful man. As was natural in that generation, he managed the household finances. Sadly, he passed away unexpectedly and she was in the dark again. The problem is, if you don't overcome your fears, really get a handle on all of your assets—what type of insurance you have, etc.—and then something happens, you're totally clueless, which is way worse than confronting your fears in the first place. It's not that you have to be in charge, but you still need to be well-informed."

Fear isn't limited to just big things like life insurance or finances. Fear caused Eileen Opatut to put off an important task, and it's likely to be a costly mistake. "A few weeks ago, I spotted this little leak in my bedroom, and today I notice that it's much, much larger. When I first saw it I ignored it because I figured getting a roofer out here is going to be really expensive. I thought, 'What if I need to replace the roof? What if there's some huge problem in the attic?' Now the leak has spread so much. I let it go too far. I should have just looked at my list and gotten it done weeks ago."

LOATHING

Not all tasks are fun. If you really hate doing something and it makes you miserable, you'll find every reason under the sun to avoid dealing with that task. Is there a task lingering on your to-do list simply because you don't like to do it?

Human Resources administrator Mary Kay McGann, soon-to-be mom and wife to south Florida radio personality Mike McCann, has a big organizational *but* when it comes to filing. "I have fallen behind on filing at home, and once it becomes a pile, it's just torture! The reason I don't ever get around to dealing with the piles is because I hate it. I'm simply terrible about motivating myself to file, at home *and* at work. The funny thing is that I will spend hours organizing my computer files both at home and at work, so it makes no sense! I guess paper files just annoy me."

Jennifer Gerace Kinkade has a similar lingering task. "I have an unfinished scrapbook, which is a long-overdue gift for someone," she says. "I just can't bring myself to do it. Why? Because I just really don't want to, it fills me with dread."

PRETTY NEAT WISDOM

BIG BUTS HOLD YOU BACK

Just like an oversized derriere will slow you down physically, an oversized organizational *but* will hold you back, too. Thinking that you're incapable of tackling something is incredibly disempowering. Excuses imply that you are a victim of circumstances and therefore powerless against your inaction. Excuses may seem to lighten your load, but they actually increase your stress load by disempowering you. And when you're feeling disempowered in one area of your life, it can spill over into another.

When you make excuses, you halt progress; you stagnate—literally slow yourself down and become duller. Stagnation isn't necessarily about doing nothing, it's about doing the same thing, again and again, without progressing. The antidote? Stop lying to yourself, take responsibility for the task, and get a move on!

For Marcy Gussin, a product manager at a large financial company, the entire notion of getting organized is a drag. "I would much rather be doing pretty much anything other than organizing things. When I get home at the end of the day I'd rather be with my important people or just vegging on the couch instead of organizing. My priorities are elsewhere. Every once in a while I'll get an organizational inspiration, but when it comes down to it I am much happier putting my energy elsewhere. I'm organized enough to function, but I still compare myself to my friends, who sure look like they've got it down perfectly. Every few months, I'll go all out and that makes me feel great, but doing it every day, even for just ten minutes, ughh ... that sounds miserable."

TIME FOR SOME BUT-BUSTING

In this section, our goal is to transform you into your own organizational personal trainer. Your mission: to eradicate your flabby excuses once and for all and reveal the superefficient, less-stressed individual you're capable of becoming. Take a cue from some of the women we interviewed who accepted responsibility for their buts and did something about them.

DARCY OVERCOMES TAX-PREP EXCUSES

While Darcy Ahl, a busy working mom with three teenagers, feels "super-organized" in most parts of her life, she admits to battling procrastination in some areas. "I feel absolutely overwhelmed by financial tasks, like preparing for tax time. For a long time, it just wasn't getting done until the last possible minute. I finally figured out that I needed a system. Now I keep a big neon envelope on my desk and I just stuff every tax-related paper into it. I don't spend time sorting it or making a perfect system, but when it's time to do my taxes, everything is together and ready to go. My system—even though it's so basic—is a lifesaver!"

LEXIE TACKLES AN EPIC MOVE

Big dreams take many forms, and when Lexie Watson married Christopher five years ago, she took on his lifelong dream of moving to Japan. "From the time I first met Chris, he talked about living in Japan. But it's not like you can pick up and move across the world tomorrow—we had jobs, a family. The logistics were overwhelming. It seemed so big to him that he just wrote it off as a fantasy, but I didn't want him to give up so easily on a dream I knew he really cared about. So we sat down and laid out the steps we'd have to take to make his dream a reality. Our goal was to move to Japan within five years of being married, and we moved there after just two-and-a-half years."

How did Lexie and Chris do it? She explains how they broke things down. "We wrote down the individual steps in a formal document. Task one was to identify how much money we'd need to save to make the move and then implement a plan to salt away what we needed each week. Task two was to identify a place to live in Japan. That involved a lot of research, because the entire country was open to us. As we dug into that task, we realized we had to figure out exactly what we wanted to get out of it. Which was more important: cultural experience, the ability to travel widely, or the ability to continue on our existing career paths? We had to learn a lot about the country to make the right choices. Other tasks on the list: language classes, visas, jobs, and establishing a social network before we arrived. It was a very long list at first, but we made it a priority to tackle one task on the list each week. Before we knew it, we were well on our way, which made it easy to get through the remaining items on the list. I have to say, the Internet was a lifesaver for us, because everything is at your fingertips."

JULIE SHEDS POUNDS WITH A WEIGHT-LOSS BUDDY

Julie Isserman is an outgoing brand manager who has struggled to stay trim for most of her life. "I have this big goal to lose thirty pounds. My fiancé is a physician, and he's supportive, but I just felt overwhelmed and totally on my own when it came to organizing the meals. So I signed up for Weight Watchers, and I got my friend Kathleen to do it with me. We work together, we prepare our healthy lunches together, and now we weigh-in together. I just couldn't reach my goal without her."

EASY AS 1-2-3

When you study people who are very good at keeping their organizational *buts* to a minimum, you realize that it's pretty easy to do.

MAKE IT A HABIT

Routines are one of the most effective but-busters out there. They're especially great for dealing with those tasks you really don't like to do. Why? Routines don't require a whole lot of brain space; they enable you to do things while on autopilot. They're also good for keeping perfectionist tendencies at bay because once you're on autopilot, you're much less likely to be hypercritical of yourself or your progress. So if you've got a *but* hanging out there, establish a morning, evening, or even midday routine to deal with it once and for all. Some suggestions:

- Make Sunday night file night (or photo organization night). Set an egg timer for thirty minutes every Sunday evening at 8:30 PM, and use that time to tackle your dreaded chore. Walk away at the end of thirty minutes with the confidence that you'll return to it again the same time next week.
- Get in the habit of doing what we like to call a "Commercial Clean." Anytime you're watching TV, take each two-minute commercial break to clean up something in the room you're in.
- Get in the habit of putting three or four things away before leaving the house. If you have a family, get everyone in the habit of doing this.

Whatever habit you want to establish, keep in mind that it takes about a month to truly establish a new one. So be vigilant with yourself (and others) during that initial time period.

TAKE BABY STEPS

If you've got a big task that you've been avoiding because you think it's too big and time-consuming, baby steps are your way to salvation. No matter how small the dent you make in a large task, the act of doing *something* to get started gets momentum working in your favor and dramatically increases your chances of taking additional steps until the job is done. Some suggestions:

- Make a dent in your home office mess by grabbing a trash bag and filling it with things you can easily throw out.
- Start cleaning out your closet by taking ten items you immediately know are outdated, have holes or stains, or no longer fit, and either toss them or donate them to charity.
- If you have lots of kid-related clutter, break down clean-up time into smaller steps and make it a game. Take a bowl and fill it with ping pong balls. Write an organizational task on each ball with a Sharpie. Set an egg timer for ten minutes. Have each child grab one ping pong ball and complete the task on it. When they're done, they come back and get another, and another, and so on. When the timer goes off, the one with the most ping pong balls wins a prize.

No matter how you decide to break down a task or problem, doing so will help you get the job done.

A PRETTY NEAT INTERVIEW

Meet: Jodie Schroeder

Family: Married with two children

Occupation: Mom

Q: What are your organizational buts?

A: My bills are my organizational buts. I really need to completely take over paying the bills from my husband, but things are just a mess right now. I have the time to do the bills and I am certainly capable, but I have a big block about doing it and it completely stresses me out. I feel like I can't do it. And I suppose if I'm honest with myself, I don't really *want* to do it either. I need to put the bills online and since I have not paid bills in ten years, this is new for me. I pay them manually right now, which is just not efficient and stresses me out.

Q: How do your buts impact your life?

A: They make things complicated and stressful. I know my friends all pay their bills online. I look at the folder of bills on my desk every day and try to stay on top of them, yet I can't get myself to start the online banking. Last week a bill slipped through the cracks and by the time I found it, it was late. The whole bill thing stresses me out and just paralyzes me for some reason.

Q: What are your organizational goals?

A: Number one is to organize all of my bills and pay them online. The second is to get my photos in albums and organize them. If I achieved those two things, it would be the equivalent of having a spotless house and a completed to-do list. It would feel fantastic!

Q: What is the most difficult part of trying to reach those goals?

A: Getting started and taking the first step is by far the most difficult part. I don't know why, but once I start, I know it will be easy to carve out the time to finish the job. That first step just seems impossible to take.

Q: Do you have any tips for others struggling to overcome their organizational buts?

A: The best thing I've ever done is to set a hard deadline to get something done. For example, I have eighteen months of pictures I want to have in photo albums. I have set a deadline of Thanksgiving to get that done so that when my family is here for the holiday, they can see all of our photos organized and in albums. Deadlines are a great motivator!

FIND A BUDDY

Why is it that tackling something you really struggle with is easier with a friend along? There's no need to go it alone—so don't! This is particularly true if you're putting something off because you're uneasy about the task and its implications (i.e., setting up an emergency plan or kit, looking into life insurance). Working with a buddy has several benefits. For example, you can help her out one week and the next week she can return the favor. Or you can work separately but hold each other accountable with a deadline or a bet, like lunch or an evening out. Being accountable to someone else is an excellent excuse buster.

CHAPTER WRAP-UP

A little procrastination is certainly normal, but unless you're vigilant, small buts can turn normal procrastination into permanent avoidance. It's important to recognize that you have buts and then work on overcoming them. There are a million reasons we make excuses about getting organized, but the fact of the matter is most will fall into one of four categories.

- *Perception vs. Reality:* when you think a job will take longer or is much bigger than it is in reality. As long as your perception is that the task is more than you can handle, it will remain undone.
- *Perfectionism:* when you're stopped in your tracks by your need for a perfect outcome. If you believe that something will never be ideally or perfectly achieved, you won't be motivated to attempt it nor persevere if you've already begun.
- *Fear:* when you're afraid of something that might happen in the future, the natural human tendency is to look for ways to escape or to avoid dealing with it. Yet avoidance and escape still leave you vulnerable.
- *Loathing:* when you truly dislike a task.

The good news is that it's easy to overcome the drivers of big organizational buts. Routines, which take up very little brain space once you've established them as habits, are a great way to tackle the tasks you loathe and keep some of your perfectionist tendencies at bay. Baby steps are the magic elixir for those jobs you're putting off because you think they're too big. And organizational buddies can help you face your fears and tackle a project you've been putting off because the topic makes you uneasy.

---

1. Jeff Beneke, "Home Storage Products Continue to Sell," About.com, December 17, 2008

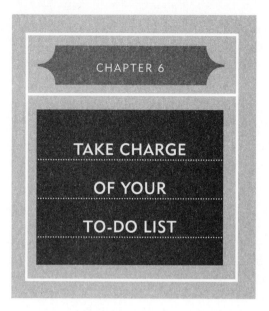

CHAPTER 6

TAKE CHARGE

OF YOUR

TO-DO LIST

"Besides the noble art of getting things done, there is the noble art of leaving

things undone. The wisdom of life consists in the elimination of non-essentials."

—LYN YUTANG

You're probably familiar with the ultra-successful "Got Milk?" campaign that ran a few years back. It featured a radio contest caller handicapped by a peanut butter sandwich, a priest in a brownie-triggered rage beating up a vending machine that won't dispense a carton of milk, and an arrogant boss who seconds after firing someone is run over by a truck and finds himself in hell, with giant chocolate chip cookies galore and a large refrigerator full of nothing but empty milk cartons. The genius of the award-winning campaign was that it perfectly captured those moments you *had to have* milk; just watching the spots made you salivate for the milk the tortured protagonist could never have.

The central theme of the campaign was uncovered using what's known in the advertising business as deprivation research. For a long time, market researchers tried to get at why people liked milk, a fairly mundane product that nearly everybody consumes at least once a day, by asking straightforward questions like, "Do you like milk? When do you like milk?" But all the answers those straightforward questions yielded were unsatisfactory, and, well, straightforward. Answers like, "It's okay." Or, "Yeah, I really like it on my cereal." To break through to a more compelling insight, researchers decided to try something radically different. They actually took milk away from people in the hopes of uncovering those moments when they absolutely, positively couldn't live without it. What the researchers found was that you crave milk most right after you eat something really rich (like peanut butter), or chocolaty (like a brownie or a chocolate chip cookie). The rest is advertising history.

We thought a lot about the technique of deprivation research when it came to the subject of to-do lists. Like milk, they're something most people keep and use pretty much every day. And like the milk researchers, our first attempts to elicit thoughts about the importance of to-do lists came up short. Perhaps it was the ordinary nature of them that made it difficult for people to put their finger on what their lists meant to them. We couldn't help but wonder what would happen if we took away our interviewees' to-do lists. Would they feel lost without them? Would they be better able to focus on the big picture?

In the end, we found we didn't have to go quite as far as taking to-do lists away. Simply mentioning deprivation research made our interviewees recoil in horror at the thought of having to operate without their lists. Nina Restieri's reaction was typical: "Oh God, if I had to go without my to-do list, it would be a disaster. I've been working with one my entire career and I don't know any other way to work. I think I would feel very chaotic. I don't know where I'd even start . . . it would be like someone taking away my cell phone. It would be that difficult for me because I don't have a naturally organized brain. If I don't have it written down on paper, it's just not going to happen." Hollie Sehrt took it one step further, saying, "If I didn't have a to-do list, my brain would probably explode. I am a visual person; I like to see what I have to do and if I couldn't see what I had to do, it would make me crazy. I wouldn't be able to sleep at night."

We knew we couldn't *really* ask the people we interviewed for this book to go without their to-do lists for a week, so as the authors, we decided to be our own guinea pigs. We made a pact to go without our lists for an entire week, doing our best to carry on with business as usual both at work and at home, and document the results. We reflected on the good and not-so-good aspects of the experience.

Q: What's it like to go without your to-do list?

A: *Sarah Welch, Buttoned Up's Chief Dreamer (SW):* Without my lists, I feel like I am missing a limb. The thought that won't stop nagging me: What am I forgetting? I keep my to-do's in a notebook with three sections: today, Buttoned Up, and personal. I make a "today" list every morning, and the other two sections are long laundry lists of to-do's. I know I've got a lot on my lists, and I'm really nervous that I will forget all of it. I'm also afraid when new to-do's pop up because I won't be able to write them down. How am I going to follow-up? What is going to get lost in the shuffle?

A: *Alicia Rockmore, Buttoned Up's Queen Bee (AR):* I hate going without my lists. It's only been twenty-four hours, and I don't know if I can make it another twenty-four! I use three legal pads—long term, weekly, and daily—and I keep them with me all the time. I've been keeping my to-do lists this way for over ten years. I guess I'm a list maniac, and I just can't survive without them.

Q: Are you better able to focus on the big picture without your list?

A: *SW:* Even though I'm stressed, I see a silver lining. Going without my to-do list is forcing me to articulate the big picture. In the morning I ask myself: What are the two most important things I have to get done today? I know I can remember at least two things (but probably not much more) all day long. With the day's important tasks in mind, I don't dilly-dally in the morning. I go straight to work on them, and that feels great.

A: *AR:* For me it's the exact opposite. I guess my lists allow the little things to be out of my mind so I can focus on the big picture. Without my lists, I am consumed with whom I need to call, which fax to send out, and I cannot think at all about the big picture.

Q: What have you learned from going without your to-do lists?

A: *SW:* For me, just the act of writing something down gets it out of my head, where it takes up space. I don't have to worry about it—even if I don't get to it for a week or two—because I know it won't be forgotten forever.

A: *AR:* I think this experience taught me two important things. First, it confirms that my three-legal-pad system is working for me. Second, I realize that I want to focus more on the big picture. Since the small things are written on my to-do list, I can forget about them and save my brain power for the big challenges that come my way. I will try not to go crazy over unimportant details as much anymore.

Deprivation interview after deprivation interview elicited the same insight: without to-do lists, interviewees were overcome by the "noise" in their head.

The real reason to do-lists are so important is that they transfer thoughts and tasks that would otherwise take up precious brain space and park them in a safe place. Think of your brain as a purse or briefcase. It has a finite amount of space. If your purse is packed to the brim, it's difficult to access the important stuff, like your phone, a pen, or your wallet when you really need them. Your brain works the same way. The simple act of transferring a task from your brain to a list frees your brain to focus on getting things done, not remembering what needs to get done.

FIND YOUR OWN WAY

There are as many ways of keeping to-do lists as there are people in the world. And that's as it should be. *How* you keep your lists isn't important. *That* you keep a list (or lists) is. No matter the format, *what you write down gets done.* According to Dave Kohl, professor emeritus at Virginia Tech, people who regularly write down their goals earn nine times as much over their lifetimes as people who don't. Think about that for a moment. No matter how lofty or simple your goals may be, reaching them requires a systematic approach. And that begins by writing your to-do list down; don't just think it, ink it!

Whether they kept their list(s) electronically, on paper, on sticky notes, or on color-coded index cards, the people we interviewed used a variety of techniques to structure their lists in a way that enabled them to progress through them more effectively and efficiently.

MASTER YOUR DETAILS

For some, particularly those who are detail oriented, keeping every item on one master list is the key to success. Compiling everything in one place works for them. Others with a penchant for detail break their to-do's down even further, distilling their master lists into categories. Whatever the method, detail-oriented people pay attention to every little thing. No matter how miniscule something is it won't escape notice.

Alissa Lippman, a meticulous stay-at-home mom expecting her second child, explains her preference for a master list. "I keep one running to-do list, even if it gets quite long. That way I know I have everything I need in one place. When I look at it, I find comfort in the fact that I can see everything I have to do; I know I haven't forgotten or 'lost' anything. I mark my priorities by starring the important things. That way I know the important stuff will get done first."

Lacey Pappas is also a fan of keeping one master list. "Keeping one master list in my planner works for me because my calendar and all of my notes are right there, too. I would feel lost and flustered without it that way."

For others, keeping one master list is too overwhelming, so they break the big list into more manageable chunks and keep those either in one notebook or on separate pieces of paper. This technique seems to work well for big-picture thinkers who need more of a narrative to their lists.

Michelle Bauman is an attorney and a mother of two who recently started her own personal coaching business. She divides her to-do list into four categories, a system she adapted from something she read about. She explains, "For me, keeping it simple doesn't mean one master list; it means categories that match my life. I keep four to-do lists: (1) a "next action" list, (2) a "waiting for" list, (3) a project list, and (4) a "maybe someday" list. It helps me stay on top of things and set priorities each day. Next actions and projects come first while the other two lists are on the back burner. I've adapted an already existing system to suit my needs; I think that's inevitable no matter which approach you choose."

Alison Lord also uses categories that match her life to help her organize her list. "If I have a lot of things to do, which is usually the case, I'll group to-do's by category and write them down in different areas of my to-do notebook page. For example, I keep one area on a page for listing all the people I need to touch base with, another area might be for an event I am planning, like my sister's wedding, and still another for my work to-do's. I'll mix in notes as needed—keeping them in their allotted area. And when the page gets too busy and full, I fold down the top corner and start a new page."

Remember, there is no right or wrong way to go about listing your to-do's. The point is to organize the to-do's so that you crank through them more efficiently.

HARNESS TODAY'S TECHNOLOGY

Earlier we articulated the golden benefit of to-do lists: what you write down gets done. But in this modern day, the word *write* can easily be replaced with the word *type*. For some, technology has transformed the way they keep track of their lists.

Marci Miller, completely relies on technology. Not only does it keep her on top of her responsibilities, but it also keeps her family in the loop about important events. She explains how technology makes life much easier. "I found that I was always losing slips of paper, so I don't write down my to-do list at all anymore. Instead, I've gone completely electronic. I have a Mac, so I use iCal, which has a calendar and a to-do list feature that I sync to my Blackberry. Everything is on it, and I set the alarms to remind me of things I need to get done according to deadline dates and priorities. My iCal is my brain; I would forget everything without it! I can keep my husband, Shawn, in the loop by sharing my list with him and by inviting him to specific events. If I just wrote those events on the kitchen calendar, I'd never know if he actually saw it, but with the electronic invite, he can respond easily. With four kids and busy schedules, technology, when it works, is a lifesaver."

Some people are a little bit paper and a little bit techno. Relying completely on technology is too much for them. Denny Ticker, an empty nester and school administrator, is a perfect example. She explains, "I'd say that I dabble in electronic organization, but I haven't given up my paper-and-pen ways. For example, my daughter loaded everyone's birthdays onto my computer's Outlook calendar, and I love that because reminders pop up a week in advance. But it works because it's a one-time thing and I don't have to do anything on a daily basis to keep it up. That said, I still want everything— especially my to-do list—written down. I can carry it with me everywhere, and I get such satisfaction out of crossing things off my list. I just don't think hitting delete would give me the same sense of accomplishment."

There is no doubt that the digital tools available for organization have radically changed the way many of us live our lives, and that includes the way we approach organization. To decide whether paper, technology, or a combination of the two is right for you, consider some key questions.

- What am I trying to accomplish with this technology?
- Am I comfortable learning to use technology?
- Are those in my inner circle tech savvy as well?
- Is this technology mobile or will I be tied to my computer?

It's important to be wary of the overpromise of technology. Today, electronic widgets are presented to us as solutions. We expect them to do the hard work for us. Just plug in the device, start using it, and *voila!*—your tasks are seamlessly integrated with your schedule . . . right? If only! Sarah reminds us that while technology can be helpful, it is just a tool that still takes time and effort on our part.

ESCAPE YOUR TO-DO LIST RUT

If you're currently stuck in a to-do list rut and searching for a fresh approach, take a cue from others who tweaked their to-do list habits to good effect.

AMY GRABOW'S SWITCH

"A paper to-do list used to work perfectly for me. But when little scraps of paper started to take over, I got a 5 x 7-inch spiral notebook with pockets to hold everything—all of my lists. It started as my grocery list, but it morphed into something much more. It has become my everything list and it's my only list. Pajamas for the girls, swim goggles, anything for the house goes on the list, and the pockets in the back hold coupons, receipts, and important notes. My everything notebook lives in the kitchen, but I always take it with me when I go somewhere, whether it's to work or the shopping mall."

HOLLY BOHN'S BIG TASK BREAKDOWN

"I'm a to-do list fanatic, but I had one big problem: Large tasks would just sit on my list forever. Because they took up the same amount of space on my list, I could just ignore them while all the little stuff got crossed off. Now I make sure to break down big tasks into manageable parts. Then my daily to-do list only has what I can reasonably get done in a day. The best part is that those big, scary projects are actually getting done this way."

ROSEMARY BIAGIONI'S ELECTRONIC ADDITION

"At work I keep a spiral notebook where I write down what I have to do every day. I never really kept lists at home because it was pretty easy for me to remember what I had to get done. If I really needed to, I'd jot down one or two personal things in my work notebook. Then my boys reached college age and that all changed. Colleges bombard you with financial aid information packets, applications, and deadlines, so it's easy to get overwhelmed. Now, every January or February I create a Microsoft Excel spreadsheet for all the college financial aid paperwork. It's a master checklist of everything that needs to get filled out, signed, submitted, etc. It's worked well for me, especially now that I have *two* in college."

As we've said before, there is no right or wrong way to keep a to-do list. The important thing is to land on a system that works for you. Once you've figured out how your to-do list will be organized, it's time to find the tools that will help you put it in play.

TO-DO LIST TECHNOLOGY

These days, it seems there are just as many options out there for electronically tracking your to-do's as there are tasks on your list! We thought it might be helpful to compare the organizational features of a few different programs and gadgets, but we encourage you to do your homework before investing in an electronic organizer. Look for gadgets with a free trial so that if it doesn't fit your needs you can ditch it for something that does.

GADGET	COST & TYPE	SHARE WITH OTHER PEOPLE?
APPLE iCAL	Comes loaded on Apple computers ($499 for iPad to $999 and up for regular computer models)	Yes
MICROSOFT OUTLOOK	$109.95 suggested retail price for MS Outlook 2007. Also comes as part of MS Office Suite ($299 and up)	Yes
GOOGLE CALENDAR	Free Web-based service	Yes
WWW.TADALIST.COM	Free Web-based service	Yes
APPLE iPHONE	$200 smart phone	Yes. IF your master calendar is synced to other calendar, such as iCal or Google Calendar
BLACKBERRY	$150–$300 smart phone	Yes. IF your master calendar is synced to other calendar, such as Google Calendar

TACKLE YOUR TO-DO'S INTELLIGENTLY

When to-do lists are long—and from what people told us, they are—most of us end up working harder instead of working smarter. Most people we spoke to along the way said they felt overwhelmed by long laundry lists and felt that priorities were slipping through the cracks. They found that what they were doing day in and day out often had more to do with deadlines than importance. The good news is that a few simple tweaks to your to-do list can do wonders to align your actions with your real priorities.

SYNC WITH OTHER GADGETS?	ORGANIZATIONAL FEATURES	EASE OF USE
Yes	Basic to-do list Alarms for scheduled appointments Color-coded calendars (e.g., "work" and "home")	Very easy to use
Yes	Integrated contacts, email, and calendar Basic task list Drag and drop emails into calendar makes follow-up easy	Easy to use, although some training required to get the most out of advanced features
Yes	Can create and view multiple calendars at once (great for families)	Easy to use
No	Create a list, add tasks to it, and share if you want to. Create as many different lists as you want.	Very easy to use
Yes, very easy if you sync to other devices, especially via MobileMe	Basic to-do list Hundreds of "Apps" available from the App Store, including: Remember the Milk, Evernote, Teuxdeux	Depends on the app you are using. Most are very straightforward
Yes, syncs with Outlook and other mail/contact programs	Task list, memo pad. Hundreds of Apps available including Evernote and Remember the Milk	Easy to use. Great for people who compose long emails or texts because it has a keyboard.

POSITION YOUR BIG THREE UP TOP

In Chapter 2, we emphasized the importance of articulating your true priorities and big picture goals, and incorporating them into your daily routines. Your to-do list is where the rubber meets the road. So it's natural that making space at the top of your list for your real priorities, deadline driven or not, is a fantastic way to keep them in the forefront, and they're more likely to get done.

Julie Isserman, who works in marketing for Frito Lay, writes her long-term goals at the top of her to-do list, which helps her focus on them. Julie explains, "I consider my priorities to be part of my to-do list. Even if they're big picture, like planning a product launch at work, they have a special place on my list. I know I won't get to cross them off immediately, but having them written down helps me focus on them. Of course when smaller things come up, I add them to my list. But my eye is always on the big picture because it's right in front of me. When I have to make a decision about how to spend my time, I see which task ties into the big picture best."

IDENTIFY "DO NOT DISTURB" TASKS

When we interviewed Lexie Watson, an interpreter for an international finance company, she talked about her tendency to start with what's most urgent and not with what's most important. That was, until her new office phone system came with a great feature: a "not-ready" button. "My ringing phone is the best example of something urgent, but not necessarily important, intruding and often interrupting work on something critical. It wants to be answered *right now*! That's hard to resist in the moment. But the beauty of this feature is that now I can set my not-ready button, and it won't ring until I'm ready for it. The important stuff gets done with undivided attention, and then I move on to that missed phone call. I look at it this way: A missed phone call can be returned without a problem later on, but a botched translation has much bigger implications for everyone."

Some tasks, like emptying the dishwasher or picking up toys, can be done on autopilot. Others require focus and attention. If you attempt to multitask while working on a something that requires focus and attention, you may be working harder, not smarter. When Lexie sets her "not-ready" button to take care of her to-do list priorities, she works smarter, not harder.

According to Dr. Gloria Marks of the University of California Irvine, it usually takes between six and twenty minutes to recover focus after an interruption. Another study carried out by the British Institute of Psychiatry on behalf of Hewlett Packard found that excessive use of technology reduced workers' intelligence, and that those distracted by incoming email and phone calls saw a ten-point fall-off in their IQ—more than twice the impact of cigarette smoking or marijuana use![1] So the math of multitasking just doesn't add up. Rather than getting more done in less time, you'll get less done in more time, and it won't be done very well.

SARAH'S TO-DO LIST TRIPLE-HEADER

Recently, *Pretty Neat* co-author Sarah Welch realized she was in a to-do list rut, so she decided to update her methods. She used to write a fresh list every day, usually in her datebook, but found that two things were making her feel frustrated: Carrying over so many tasks from day to day was a pain, and staring at her never-shrinking list made her feel overwhelmed. Switching it up, she says, was as easy as 1-2-3.

"I start by writing all my to-do's in a spiral notebook, where I can be messy and the list can be *loooong*. Then I write down my top three priorities from that list in my datebook. I love just writing three things in the morning that I *have* to do. It's so much easier to focus and get going when I only have three things on the list. I usually tear through those pretty quickly and then transfer another set of three to my datebook list from my master list. But if I don't, I don't feel like a failure!

"I also like keeping a master list in a non-fancy notebook. That way, when I've crossed off enough of the master list, I can rip out the old list and throw it away without feeling like I'm wrecking anything. I would never be able to do that with a fancy journal."

Identify tasks on your to-do lists, particularly high priority ones, and literally write "DND" (do not disturb) next to them. When it's time to work on DND items, let your phone calls go to voice mail, turn off the incoming mail alert in your email program, and focus on the task at hand. If you know you'll need to escape other interruptions, identify a quiet place you can go to work on something, like a coffee shop or an unused office down the hall. Getting in the habit of identifying DND tasks and treating them differently will increase the likelihood that you'll get them done in less time, with less stress.

WARM UP TO BIG TASKS

Many experts advise people to tackle their to-do list in priority order. That is, start with the most important task and work your way down the list. In theory, that makes a lot of sense. Even if you're not able to make too much of a dent in your list, at least you'll have crossed off the most important. In reality, diving in and taking on a high priority but complex task first may not be the best approach. Sometimes, a little warm up is in order. Using a sports analogy, if you're a professional sprinter, sprint drills are a high priority part of your daily training regimen. But you wouldn't ever do your sprint drills cold, the moment you walked onto the field. You warm your body up to get your blood pumping, muscles working, and heart rate going. Diving straight into sprints could cause an injury.

When it comes to your to-do's, give yourself some warm-up activities; tasks lingering on your list that don't take much effort to complete and cross off. Warm-up tasks might be quick phone calls, returning a few emails, or paying bills. By starting small, you build momentum, and ultimately get the principle of organizational inertia to work in your favor. A body in motion will stay in motion, and it's easier to get a body *not* in motion to start moving if the task at hand is easy.

Julie Isserman summarized how organizational inertia works for her. "I buy into the theory of organizational inertia. Once I get started on my to-do list, I just cruise right through it. But I've got to start off small. The important thing is for me to pick one or two little tasks that I can quickly cross off. That gets me going and motivates me to get to the big stuff next."

Of course, this rule should be used carefully. Don't use it as an excuse to get the unimportant stuff done while avoiding your priorities. We recommend you do this by limiting yourself to one or two quick tasks and by giving yourself a time limit. If a task that was supposed to be quick and easy exceeds your time limit, then put it aside so that you can tackle what really matters.

KEEP YOUR TO-DO LIST UP-TO-DATE

Your life is always changing, and your to-do list should change with it. In fact, if your list stops changing, then you've either stopped using it or you've stopped accomplishing things on your list. Neither option is very productive. A great way to keep your to-do list up-to-date is by establishing daily and weekly routines.

ESTABLISH A DAILY ROUTINE

Pick a specific time of day, whether it's first thing in the morning or last thing in the evening, and go through your current to-do list and either revise it or make a new one. If you're not in the habit of doing this already, try it for the next thirty days. You'll find that taking five or ten minutes to put your list together, pick priorities, set DND times, and identify warm-up tasks will dramatically increase your productivity.

Susan Bachtelle is a busy accountant living in Southern California. She established a daily routine to keep her to-do's organized. "I make my to-do list every morning as soon as I get to work. I try to make it realistic so that

I'll be able to get it done in a day, and I make a point to revise it in the afternoon. My list is really always in a state of revision as new things come up at work, but setting aside time twice a day ensures that I can keep up. If I didn't have this routine, I wouldn't keep up with the important stuff."

Leah Ticker, a first-grade teacher living in Los Angeles, uses an evening routine to clear her head before bed. "I am not a morning person, so I take time in the evening to prepare myself for the next day. I pack my bag, lay out my clothes, and go over the next day's to-do list. I review priority tasks and make appointments in my calendar to tackle those, and I try to make those appointments in quieter times of the day when I know I won't be interrupted. I also started keeping a pen and paper on my bedside table. If I can't get to sleep because something is nagging me, or a must-do thought wakes me up at night, I jot it down. I find that I wake up with a sense of purpose and direction now that I have this routine. I know what I have to do, and when I have to do it."

DO A WEEKLY REVIEW

Weekly to-do list routines give you an opportunity to step back, view the big picture, and break big picture tasks down into daily to-do's. If you don't already have a weekly routine, set aside ten minutes on Sunday nights for the next month and use that time to identify long-term priorities or big projects, then break them into smaller tasks that can be done throughout the week, and integrate them into your daily to-do list.

Holly Bohn works full time, and her sons, ages ten and twelve, keep her busy at home. Her work list and personal list are one and the same. "My life is seamless, and I need to be on top of both work and home at all times. To keep all those plates spinning, I sort my to-do's by week and by day. Every Sunday, I break down larger tasks into pieces that I can accomplish. The bigger task remains on my weekly list, while the smaller pieces make it onto the daily list. My to-do list is never-ending, but my routine makes it a little more manageable."

CHAPTER WRAP-UP

To-do lists are important because they transfer thoughts and tasks that take up precious brain space and park them in a safe place. They free your brain to focus on getting things done. Although it doesn't matter how you keep your to-do's, there are a variety of techniques and technologies that can help you progress through your list more effectively and efficiently.

Meet: Sarah Merz

Family: Single

Occupation: President and CEO of FranklinCovey

Sarah Merz is a very busy woman. As president of FranklinCovey, a leader in time-management products and training, Sarah knows that organization is crucial to success. She balances a demanding professional life with her personal pursuits, and she is well on her way to reaching her goal of running 365 miles this year.

Q: What role does organizing play in your life?

A: Organizing is important to me because there's a direct correlation between how organized I am and how clearly I think. When I'm disorganized, I'm stressed. I guess I've always been that way, but it's definitely increased over the years. I think there's a certain level of accuracy and order necessary for success.

Q: You have a special way of keeping your to-do list. Can you tell us about it?

A: My personal list and my work list are one and the same, and I've got a trick that keeps me from overextending myself. It works like this: I use a page in my small day planner, so I've got a limited amount of space to start. That's important, not pages and pages of to-do's. My professional list goes at the top of my to-do list page and I work my way downward. My personal list starts at the bottom and goes up. I try to keep some space between the two lists. If the two lists get close to meeting in the middle, it probably means the list has gotten too long for me to manage it all. This system keeps me from biting off more than I can chew.

Q: With your busy schedule, how do you make "you time" a priority on your to-do list?

A: I think everyone should schedule "me time" into their calendar. So often, the way I get "me time" is by scheduling an event that involves somebody else—a facial, working out with a trainer, a massage, going for a run with a friend. Because another person is counting on me, I have to consider it just like any other appointment. Not only do I schedule "me time" into my monthly calendar, but I keep track of completed appointments with a colored dot so I can see if I've had enough "me time" in a given month.

Q: Do you have any other advice to share?

A: Routines. They are a great way to do things on autopilot. I don't want to waste brain cells on stuff that should be part of my routine. I want my mind free to think about important stuff. I am a creature of habit, and it really serves me well.

- *Find Your Own Way:* If you're a detail-oriented person, nothing escapes your eagle eye, so keeping your to-do's on one master list works well. If you're more of a big picture type, consider organizing tasks into more manageable chunks under separate categories that reflect the narrative of your life.
- *Harness Today's Technology:* If you respond well to stimuli like alarms, keeping track of your to-do's using software makes a lot of sense. Technology also makes it much easier to sync your tasks and to-do's with others, which can be terrific for busy families.
- *Escape Your To-Do List Rut:* If you're currently stuck in a to-do list rut and searching for a fresh approach, tweak your to-do list habits. There is no right or wrong way to keep a to-do list. The important thing is to land on a system that works for you.
- *Position Your Big Three Up Top:* Making space at the top of your list for your real priorities, deadline driven or not, is a fantastic way to keep them in the forefront, and they're more likely to get done.
- *Identify "Do Not Disturb" Tasks:* Identify tasks on your to-do lists, particularly high priority ones that require concentration and thought and write "DND" next to them. When it's time to work on DND items, let your phone calls go to voice mail, turn off the incoming mail alert in your email program, and focus on the task at hand.
- *Warm Up to Big Tasks:* When it comes to tackling your to-do list each day, give yourself one or two warm-up activities. These should be tasks on your list that don't take much effort to complete. They get momentum working in your favor, which makes it easier to tackle larger, more important tasks.
- *Establish Daily and Weekly Routines:* Pick a specific time of day, whether it's first thing in the morning or last thing in the evening, and go through your current to-do list Revise it or make a new one. Then, once a week, step back, identify longer-term priorities or big projects, then break them into smaller tasks that can be done throughout the week and integrate them into your daily to-do's.

---

1. BBC News, "Infomania Worse Than Marijuana," April 22, 2005.

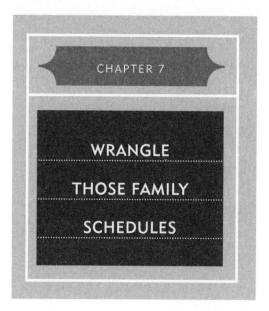

CHAPTER 7

WRANGLE
THOSE FAMILY
SCHEDULES

"There cannot be a crisis today; my schedule is already full."

—HENRY KISSINGER

Cram-packed schedules are something that literally *everybody* experiences. Your life, as you well know, is much too busy. It's crunch time at work. You promised to drop off dinner to your friend with the new baby. Your in-laws are in town. You've got ten minutes to get from the office to your son's recital. And your PDA insists on reminding you of all of this by incessantly buzzing, every five minutes.

We call this "scheduled madness." And based on the hundreds of interviews we conducted with people, most of us have it bad.

So what can you do? Option 1: Give in to the madness. After all, your schedule is packed with important stuff—some of which you can control a little or a lot, and some of which you can't control at all. Option 2: You can take a deep breath, make some tough choices, and come to terms with the fact that you and your busy family need a new plan.

You need a better schedule. We're not talking about a revolution. Don't burn your Blackberry, ignore deadlines at work, or drop the in-laws at the airport three days early. That's called *under*scheduling, and it is "scheduled madness," too. Schedules are a great thing. In fact, our research tells us that people who make schedules and manage to stick to them get more done and feel more accomplished. Unfortunately, scheduled madness has the opposite effect. It stresses you out. It makes you feel out of control. It compromises your ability to do well the things you really want to get done.

ONE SIZE DOES NOT FIT ALL

Schedules are powerful tools. They help us reach our goals. They make sure we don't miss out on important events. They keep us and, if we have them, our families running smoothly, and more important, running sanely. But when it comes to schedules, one size does not fill all. We want you to meet four women whose lives may be very different, but they share one thing in common: They all struggle with scheduling.

Every member of Cherell Jordin's young family has a hectic schedule. Cherell and her husband both work full-time and travel frequently for their jobs. They also compete in triathlons and train together at least fourteen hours a week. Their two children both play sports and participate in after-school activities several days a week. Making it all work together—and carving out ample family time—is like conducting a symphony. Cherell explains, "Sometimes our schedule is just packed. It really gets complicated, especially when I travel, and it's kind of a miracle that we all make it through the week."

Juggling busy schedules during marriage is hard, and it only gets tougher after a divorce. Kim Yorio, who owns and runs a public relations firm in New Jersey, learned this firsthand when she separated from her husband last year. "My ex-husband and I share custody of our nine-year-old son, and scheduling is a challenge, to say the least. It's not that my son's schedule is packed with a million activities or anything. But since the divorce, I have to be so much more deliberate in planning—even for basic stuff. And any changes to the schedule have to be okay with my ex as well. No more last-minute plans. It's a tough adjustment."

Just as scheduling is difficult for couples that separate, it's also a challenge for those who are just starting out together. When Megan Lipschultz moved in with her boyfriend, David, they had to adjust to very different schedules. "Right after we got our place together, David got this amazing opportunity to direct a sports newscast for the NFL Network. He loves his job—except for the 4:00 AM call time on game day. Plus, his days off are Monday and Tuesday because he works all weekend long. My schedule is a traditional nine-to-five one, with the occasional work evening here and there. That means we only have time together on Sunday afternoons. We try to make the best of it, but it's definitely not ideal."

The single life isn't without its scheduling challenges either. Megan Chin is a pediatric dentist with a busy professional and personal life. "When I moved from New York to Los Angeles to do my dental residency at UCLA, I was thrilled to be back in sunny California. But between my residency at a dental clinic serving low-income families, and the load of coursework at UCLA, I never have time to enjoy my friends or the beach. And I feel like my single status is a disadvantage: My schedule is the worst, plus my colleagues at the clinic assume my availability is 100 percent. I'm always the first person they ask to cover for them when a 'family event' comes up, and I feel terrible saying no. Who am I to keep someone from their daughter's third birthday party? It's frustrating. I may be single, but I have a schedule too!"

TAKING STOCK

As Cherell, Kim, and both Megans can attest, effective scheduling is tough stuff. The consequences of getting it right are significant. When schedules are off, the resulting stress and chaos turns even the most laid-back among us into crabbier, less creative versions of our usual selves. Worse, ineffective scheduling steals from us the only thing that matters: the present moment. Anyone who has been physically present at an event, like their child's piano recital, but mentally ten thousand miles away because they're worried about something else they should be doing, has had the present moment stolen from them. You never get those moments back.

If you're frustrated with your current approach to scheduling, the crucial question to ask yourself is: What do I change? Admittedly, when you're out of scheduling sorts, that question isn't easily answered. Why? Because you're too busy chasing your tail to stop and see the forest for the trees. A great way to get some perspective is to think about your most significant scheduling pain points. Are they related to communication with others, or complexity and overload? To help you frame your issues, we've put together the quiz

IDENTIFYING SCHEDULING PAIN POINTS

Carefully read the statements below and consider how well each one describes your schedule. Use the following scale to evaluate the statements.

1 = My schedule is always like this
2 = My schedule is regularly like this
3 = My schedule is a little like this
4 = My schedule is nothing like this

Don't look at the statements as good or bad. Your job is to reflect on what you're doing now and determine whether you've got one major scheduling issue to tackle, or many.

1. Only one person is in charge of keeping the family schedule.
2. The kids' schedule is my schedule; they are one and the same.
3. I do not have a formal process for sharing my calendar with others and vice versa.
4. Some people in my household keep track of their schedules with pen and paper while others rely exclusively on technology.
5. Everybody in my household uses technology to keep track of their schedules, but the programs are not synced to a master calendar.
6. I live with at least one other person and we do not discuss our schedules on a regular basis.
7. Once something gets scheduled on my calendar or someone else's, it's not clear whose responsibility it is to ensure everything goes smoothly on that day (e.g., people have the right uniforms with them, carpools have been arranged, etc.).
8. Schedules in my household change frequently, so it's hard to know what the latest schedule really is.

SCORING KEY:

Questions 1–2: If you put a 1 or a 2 next to these questions, you are likely to have what we call "point person overload."

Questions 3–6: If you put a 1 or a 2 next to any of these questions, syncing calendars is a real challenge for you.

Question 7: If you put a 1 or a 2 next to this question, you need more help coordinating the details that go along with scheduled activities.

Question 8: If you put a 1 or a 2 next to this question, you have an upkeep issue.

below, which will help you identify the extent to which you have problems in four major areas. Take a few minutes now to take stock.

Where did you net out? Do you have one major pain point, or many? If it's the latter, don't beat yourself up! It's not unusual for people to struggle with multiple issues when it comes to scheduling. Remember, it's tough stuff. Our goal is to get you on track, and we aim to do that by showing you how other busy, frazzled people have overcome these issues and gotten the hang of scheduling.

In our travels, we've found that people routinely struggle with scheduling in four main areas: point person overload, syncing with others, coordinating activity details, and controlling constant schedule changes. In that spirit, we've organized the rest of the chapter along those lines. For each problem area, we provide some color on what it is and why it tends to be an issue. Then we spell out effective road-tested strategies for overcoming it.

POINT PERSON OVERLOAD

In most households, one person is primarily responsible for the schedules (hint: more often than not, it's a she). That's true whether you have children or not. When you think about it, having one central point person does make sense. If no one takes charge of coordinating between family members or roommates, you're more likely to be like ships passing in the night, missing opportunities to connect and create new shared experiences. Once you add kids to the mix, having a point person becomes absolutely essential. Children depend entirely on grownups to fill their schedules with meaningful activities and shuttle them to and fro. If no one takes ownership of their schedules, the result is pure chaos.

When you're the primary person responsible for managing the schedules of multiple people, each juggling multiple responsibilities, it can easily lead to overload. Naturally, the more schedules you have to manage, or at least coordinate, the more intense the problem.

1. CREATE A SCHEDULE STATION (REAL OR VIRTUAL)

Effective scheduling requires a system that is accessible to everyone. The more others can refer to a system, the less they have to rely on you for every little detail, and the less overloaded you'll be. The first step is to establish a schedule station. It can be a real station, like a whiteboard in the kitchen; or a virtual one, like a shared Google Calendar. If you choose a virtual system, make sure that every family member syncs their individual calendars to it and checks it on a daily basis. Otherwise, you don't have a schedule station!

If you choose a physical set-up, make sure it is in a high traffic spot, like the kitchen, the front hall, or the family room. This way family members will see it at least once a day, which dramatically increases the likelihood that they will use it. Whether you choose to use a whiteboard or a paper calendar, your schedule station should also have a bulletin board next to the main calendar. Many extracurricular activities and school missives are still printed on paper, and you'll find that it's easier to keep track of them if you post them in a central location. Before you hammer a single nail, make sure it's accessible to everyone; eye-level for a seven-year-old looks a little different than that of an adult. Hang it in a spot that is easy enough for you to update and yet still visible to kids. Once that's set, be sure to have supplies like pens, thumbtacks, and magnets on hand.

There's no right or wrong way to set up a scheduling station. Below are a few road-tested set-ups to get you started.

Nina's momAgenda

Nina Restieri, creator of momAgenda and mother to four, actually launched a business aimed at helping women just like her overcome point person overload. "The momAgenda exists because I am so disorganized. I was such a mess with my four kids. I tried regular planners and never seemed to be able to get those formats to work for me. So I created my own. The momAgenda journal layout enables anyone looking at the calendar to see everyone else's calendar on a day-by-day basis. I take it with me whenever I'm out, but at home it lives on my kitchen counter. Everyone in the family is used to looking at it before checking in with me. They're really well trained. My kids and husband look stuff up for themselves all the time, and they're great about checking to make sure their social stuff is written down there. It's great."

Rachel and Leah's "Home Office"

Rachel Mahgerefteh has been living with her roommate, Leah, for almost three years. "We've got busy schedules with work and friends, and Leah travels a lot, so sometimes we'll go days without seeing each other. More than once, I've called her frantically at midnight only to discover she's actually out of town. So when we moved into a new apartment last year, we set up a corner of the living room with a bookshelf, a bulletin board, and a calendar. We joke that it's our 'office' and it works great as a schedule station. We leave each other notes, and we fill in the calendar with anything that might be of interest, like trips, parties, and when we're having out-of-town guests. It's a great way for us to connect, even if our schedules don't match up."

Marci's Techno Solutions

Marci, busy mom to four, has found that technology is a great way to keep the family schedules humming. She explains, "With four children I'm always on the move. Technology is really the best way to keep everything straight. I wouldn't think of leaving the house without my Blackberry phone, so I never have to worry whether I've left the house without my calendar. I keep a master schedule on my home computer and on my Blackberry and sync all of them multiple times a day. My husband, who is a busy entrepreneur, is also a bit of a tech geek, so the techno approach is really the only way I can be sure he engages at all with the schedule. I send him calendar invitations for events he needs to attend. If he accepts, which takes one mouse click, the appointment is automatically logged into his master calendar so he and his assistant can schedule around it."

2. HAVE CLEAR RULES OF ENGAGEMENT

Once you have a schedule station set up, it's time to train your troops. Be explicit about your expectations. Rule number one should be: Check the schedule first before coming to me. Let everyone know that all sports schedules will be written on the calendar or posted on the virtual family calendar. They are to consult the calendar before they come to you to ask what time the soccer game is on Tuesday. The same holds true for special requests, like sleepovers.

A Pretty Neat Tip

CHERELL'S WHITEBOARD

Everyone in Cherell's family has a busy schedule—jobs, frequent travel, triathlon training, sports and school for the little ones. The trick that made all the difference for her: going low-tech.

"I organize myself with technology at work; my iPhone and Outlook are great for me," she explains. "But my kids can't work with that. We needed a good, old-fashioned calendar. So in the mudroom, we put up a magnetic bulletin board and a big white-board calendar. The bulletin board has notes from school, invitations to parties, and coupons that relate to things on the calendar. Next to it is the calendar, and everything for everyone gets written on the calendar. There's a color for each family member, and that is great for the kids because they can see what is written in their color for that day."

3. DELEGATE

If you are handling all of the scheduling for you, your family, even the pets, it might be time to consider delegating some of this job to others in the family. We have found that there are usually discrete categories that you can give to others to handle that can significantly free up your time, not to mention your energy. Consider, for example, letting your spouse handle all the plans regarding his extended family. Why do you need to pick dates and make the plane and hotel reservations to visit his parents? You don't. Just delegate it. Older kids (ten and up) can handle keeping a master calendar, kept in a central place or electronically, for sports teams and after-school activities that only they participate in. You can help them manage things like who will pick them up and then call to confirm plans.

GETTING IN SYNC

Have you ever headed out the door in the morning, cheerily assuming that everyone understood where they needed to be that day, only to discover later, when people didn't show up when and where they were supposed to, that you were delusional? One of the most difficult aspects of scheduling is ensuring that each person is clued in to both their own agenda *and* the big picture. If your team isn't in sync, disappointment and frustration are inevitable; someone will miss an important event, end up in the wrong place at the wrong time, or feel shortchanged because nobody showed up to support them at their game or event.

When you have a busy household, how do you get others in the habit of syncing calendars? What's the secret? It's not rocket science. It just requires a little trial and error and then establishing some new habits.

1. HOLD REGULAR FAMILY MEETINGS

Schedules don't mean much if everybody in the household marches to the beat of their own drum. The most effective way to ensure that everybody is on the same page is to hold regular family meetings. These can be as formal or informal as you want. They shouldn't be long—five minutes is more than enough. All you need in these meetings is to ensure that you get the latest information from everyone. Then quickly go through the upcoming week and highlight conflicts (for example, two events scheduled at the same time) and agree together on the best way to resolve those conflicts.

If you know your family will roll their eyes and veto any family schedule meeting, try one of the following Jedi mind tricks to get them to see the light.

If everyone on the schedule is over the age of ten, use a little tough love. As long as they refuse to participate in a five-minute family sync at least once a week, everybody is on their own when it comes to the schedule. That means no shuttling, no carpool arranging, and no cheering. It will be one tough week, but trust us, after one missed game or event, you'll have a group of willing participants. If you have little ones under the age of ten, continue to organize and manage their schedules as usual.

Plan to have one meal, ideally dinner on Sunday evening, at home together during the week. Bring your calendar and kick off the conversation by asking everyone about their schedules for the upcoming week. Identify conflicts and resolve them together. They won't even know they've just attended a scheduling meeting (especially if the food is a favorite, like pizza or Chinese take-out).

Here are a few additional examples of regular meetings that work.

Cherell's Bimonthly Meetings

"My husband and I have always been pretty together, but once we had kids and started training for triathlons, we absolutely had to coordinate. Now that the kids are old enough, we even include them in the process. Once or twice a month, we all sit down together and plan our schedules. We make sure everything gets put on the calendar in the mudroom, and we grown-ups add it into our electronic calendars. Family time gets scheduled in, too, because it's really important to us. It's great to have the kids involved, and I hope we're teaching them some important skills. Also, on Sunday night my husband and I take a look at the week and make our to-do lists based on the calendar. I go through periods when I feel like things are piling up, but we do a lot of scheduling and our system seems to work for us."

Susan's Daily Dinner Sync

Susan Bachtelle and her fiancé both balance busy careers and have a wedding in the works. She explains how she and her husband-to-be keep it all straight. "I am an accountant, so I have to be organized for all of my clients. It's hugely important to my job. I don't think I could live without my lists and schedules, and that is as true at home as it is at work. When it comes to scheduling, my fiancé and I discuss everything over dinner. While we're relaxing together and catching up, we share schedules and figure out what needs to get done the next day and throughout the week. It's a great way for us to make sure we're getting the important stuff done, and it still feels like quality time together. I'm sure our system will change when it's not just us and the dog, but for now, it's perfect."

2. GIVE TECHNOLOGY A TRY

Some people swear by technology, others swear it off. For every person we met who swore pen and pencil was faster and better than digital, there was another equally passionate person championing the use of technology. The right answer, of course, is to do what works for you. If you're currently using pen and paper to keep track of schedules and are constantly running into syncing issues, it may be time to test the tech waters. This is particularly true if you're trying to coordinate with teenagers or a tech savvy spouse or roommate. We've found that the most effective techno tools for syncing are electronic calendar programs and electronic reminders.

E-calendar programs come in many guises, from expensive software programs like Outlook and Entourage to free online versions like Google Calendar and Cozi. The simplest way to use one is to put the entire family schedule on an e-calendar program and "invite" family members to attend relevant events. With an online family calendar, family members can view each others' schedules simultaneously, so conflicts are easy to spot. If you and your family are confident in your tech abilities, have everyone sync their computer-based calendar program to an online calendar.

Electronic reminders also come in many guises. You can send an email to someone reminding them of a scheduling obligation. You can send them an invitation to a game or event with a reminder that will pop up on their calendar as the date approaches. Or you can text them with a reminder. To be doubly certain you've alerted them, set up a reminder appointment for yourself on your computer or handheld device (check out applications for your mobile device like iProcrastinate, Things, my Lists, and reQall, which you can download from the Apple App Store or Blackberry App World) and forward the reminder on to the other person when you are pinged.

COORDINATION HEADACHES

Even if you've created a user-friendly, accessible schedule that works for you and your family, and you've even found ways to get everyone involved in the process—you're still not done. In reality, scheduling is just the first step.

Now that you know what everyone is doing, it's time to get them organized to actually *do* it.

Consider a basic item on a typical busy family schedule: a child's soccer match. The first step is loading her practice schedule into the family schedule and syncing it to a Blackberry. That's a no-brainer. But now it's time to arrange carpools to get her from school to the field, figure out which equipment to pack in her gym bag the night before, and make sure she has a carb-loaded after-school snack with her in case she gets hungry along the way. And the final bit of schedule jujitsu: clearing your schedule to be sure you can watch her play on game day.

Scheduling naturally has lots of knock-on effects, from figuring out carpool options to packing. Dealing with all of those additional to-do's can be a headache. Happily, there are ways to streamline the next steps so that you feel less stressed and more in control.

1. BUILD ACTIVITY KITS

Regularly scheduled activities will make up the bulk of your "follow-on work" (the myriad details associated with scheduled activities), which means you can set up basic systems, or kits, that significantly streamline the coordination required. Make a list of the regular weekly activities for you and your family, then write down the items required for each activity. For example: Piano lessons require music books and a notebook. The final step is to create a space where you can store the kits (which can be anything from a labeled bag to a plastic box) so they are ready to go when you need them. Just think, no more running around trying to find the baseball glove at the eleventh hour! Obviously, anyone over the age of ten should take care of assembling their own kits.

2. EMAIL YOURSELF FOLLOW-UP TASKS

If you use Microsoft Outlook for Windows, you can translate an email into a scheduled event on your calendar. Simply send yourself an email with all of the follow-up tasks that you have to complete for an upcoming event to be successful. When you open the email, drag it to the calendar icon on your task bar and it will automatically open up an appointment for you. Voilà! Set a date and time to complete the required tasks and you're golden. No more rushing around with your hair on fire at the last minute. If you don't use Microsoft Outlook for Windows, simply set up an appointment in your calendar directly and use the notes section to outline your to-do's.

Meet: Agnes Perozzi

Family: Married with three kids

Occupation: Stay-at-home mom

Agnes is a dynamic stay-at-home mom who holds down the fort for her very busy husband, Tom, and three teenage boys. In between managing their schedules, she finds time to be a volunteer, a supportive sister, and an aunt. Here's a glimpse of how she wrangles it all so effectively.

Q: Do you keep a family schedule? If so, in what form?

A: Yes, we definitely have a master family calendar. It's a large paper one that I keep on my desk in the first-floor study. I also keep a large 'plate' in the kitchen where I write the events of the day. I got the plate at a home show and you write on it with an erasable marker—sort of like having an erasable board on the fridge. It's a great reminder of where I need to be each day.

Q: You have a busy household. Is there one person in your family that is responsible for the family calendar?

A: Since my husband travels for work a great deal and I'm a stay-at-home mom with three boys, it makes the most sense for me to be the one who manages the family calendar.

Q: What's the hardest thing about keeping your family schedule organized?

A: Taking the time to write all of the schedules on the main calendar at the beginning of the school year. There are so many different schedules: school, sports, practice, piano, religious education, dentist, eye doctor, birthdays, travel, etc. But in the end it doesn't take *that* much time to transcribe it all, and once they're all in place, I feel so much more in control—plus I can pitch the paperwork cluttering up my space.

3. SET A SUNDAY NIGHT PLAN

Set aside fifteen to twenty minutes on a Sunday evening to go through your calendar and outline what you need to prepare for the events on your schedule in the coming week. Create a daily checklist for yourself, and others if they're under ten.

Q: How do you sync schedules with other family members?

A: We keep it pretty low-tech. I look at the week and the month to see what is going on and to avoid surprises. I put everything on my master calendar, including my husband's travel schedule. My kids know to give me copies of their schedules and I usually make a copy of their athletic schedules and give one to my husband, put one on my calendar, and put a copy in my car. I then give them back their calendars so that they can keep track of their own stuff. Between the five of us, someone will know what is going on.

Q: Are you also responsible for handling all of the knock-on implications from scheduling things? For example, are you responsible for arranging carpools, ensuring your boys have the equipment they need on that day?

A: Yes, in general I am. However, the kids are responsible for having their equipment together in their bags the night before if it is a school night. They have separate bags for sports equipment/uniforms/music books/school books, which keeps the stress down. You know, I found that it just takes one missing knee pad or lack of water to make them remember the next time. My advice is to avoid bringing items they have forgotten to them after the fact. I gave my kids a two-strike rule. If they forgot something more than twice, they had to suffer the consequences. The magic is, they rarely forget things now.

Q: At what age do you think it is okay for kids to take responsibility for their personal schedules?

A: Ten or so. My children are thirteen, sixteen, and nineteen. They started keeping an assignment book in third grade. Thankfully the school taught them how to organize their homework, and I eventually had them add their other schedules to their book, and made them responsible for reminding me about what they had to do each day. Full disclosure: We got to this solution by trial and error over the span of a few years— but once we settled on this, it worked like a charm. Another factor that helps is that the kids know homework comes first. They know if they don't do well in school, they don't get to do the other things they want to do, so they're incentivized to keep track!

CONTROLLING CONSTANT SCHEDULE CHANGES

Have you ever gotten a frantic "where-are-you" phone call because your daughter forgot to tell you that her choir rehearsal moved to a different day? It's not your fault, but if she didn't have a systematic way to communicate schedule changes to you, then it's not really her fault either. The same goes for husbands, roommates, and anyone else who's sharing your life and your home. Giving your family clear expectations on how to deal with the inevitable scheduling changes that crop up will help your schedule, and your life, run smoothly.

Schedule changes are inevitable and there's really only one way to deal with them. The secret: Establish right away with your family the *one* way that schedule changes should be communicated. Having one "channel," if you will, that is designated for schedule changes means you will be significantly less likely to miss important changes. The channel you use can be as low-tech or high-tech as you want it to be, but given the last-minute nature of most schedule changes, high-tech might be the better way to go.

Angela Costley, mom to two boys, uses email to great effect. "Our schedule is constantly changing, and I have to communicate changes to everyone to avoid family meltdowns. I roll with it better than at least two members of my family—I can change direction and plans, wing it, improvise much more easily than my husband and one of my boys. The method we use is email, even though I keep the master family calendar on paper. Everyone emails me any changes and asks me if the change will work. If I say yes, I respond to all and it goes on our calendar."

Marci Miller has established texting as the de facto method for communicating schedule changes. "We've got six schedules altogether. Dustin is five; Megan is eight; Harry is eleven; and Logan is thirteen. I won't tell you how old my husband is, but I manage his schedule as well. While I am happily the household manager, I want the kids to learn to be responsible for themselves and their schedule, especially when there are last-minute changes, which there always are. I'm flexible when practice time changes or my husband has a last-minute meeting, but I just need to know. Dustin and Megan aren't that independent, but my older boys and my husband keep me posted on their whereabouts via text. It's not a perfect system, but when everyone lets me know what's up, I can quickly adjust course and don't feel like I'm going it alone."

CHAPTER WRAP-UP

Schedules are powerful tools. They help us reach our goals. They make sure we don't miss out on important events. They keep us, and if we have them, our families, running smoothly, and more important, running sanely. But getting scheduling right is tough stuff. We found that people routinely struggle with scheduling in four main areas: point person overload, syncing with others, coordinating follow-on details, and keeping up with constant changes.

- *Eliminate Point Person Overload:* Effective scheduling requires a system that is accessible to everyone. The more others can look to a system, the less they have to rely on you for every little detail, and the less overloaded you'll be. Establish a schedule station (either real or virtual) and train your troops to check the schedule first before coming to you. Finally, delegate. There is no reason you have to coordinate every single detail of everyone's schedules.

- *Get In Sync:* If your team isn't in sync, disappointment and frustration are inevitable; someone will miss an important event, end up in the wrong place at the wrong time, or feel shortchanged because nobody showed up to support them. The most effective way to ensure that everybody is on the same page is to hold regular family meetings. Spend five minutes a week to ensure you have everyone's latest information. Then highlight any scheduling conflicts (for example, two events scheduled at the same time) and agree on the best way to resolve conflicts. Technology can also be a huge help.
- *Reduce Coordination Headaches:* Scheduling naturally has lots of knock-on effects, from figuring out carpool options to packing. Create weekly activity "kits" to keep items handy for regularly scheduled activities. Put them in a separate labeled bag or plastic box so they are ready to go when you need them. Review your calendar on Sunday evenings and map out follow-ups on your to-do lists.
- *Pick* One *Way to Communicate Schedule Changes:* Changes are inevitable and will always be a part of scheduling. There's really only one way to deal with them: Establish right away with your family the *one* way that schedule changes should be communicated.

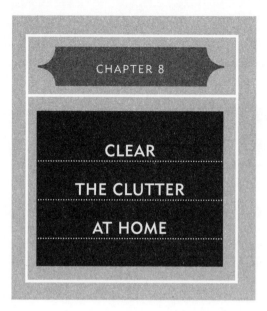

CHAPTER 8

CLEAR
THE CLUTTER
AT HOME

"Out of clutter, find simplicity."

—ALBERT EINSTEIN

Each day, people are flooded with more information, goods, services, and experiences than they can possibly consume. The onslaught makes it difficult to determine what's important to hold on to and what's not. Unfortunately, that means it doesn't take long for things to accumulate. Everybody, and we mean everybody, has a touch of Cluttertosis. It's not a problem limited to hoarders, who obviously suffer from such an extreme case that it impedes their ability to function. Clutter is simply a fact of life, and regardless of our good intentions to tame it, items have a tendency to multiply like rabbits and take up more space with each passing season.

Creating room to breathe is a crucial step to living a more organized life. A recent study revealed that clutter is one of the top three (if not the top) impediments to having a more organized home.[1] Getting rid of all that unnecessary stuff has big benefits. It can significantly reduce the amount of housework because you'll have fewer items to pick up and put away, dust, or otherwise keep orderly. Dealing with clutter can also help you reign in unnecessary spending. When your space is disorganized and overflowing with items you don't need or use, it's harder to find items you need but already have, so you waste money replacing them or buying organizational tools or even soliciting professional assistance to help you wrangle everything.

Clutter is a major stressor. When we interviewed people about clutter, time and time again they used words like "overwhelmed," "nightmare," and "guilty" to describe how they felt about the issue. People who were generally on top of it felt as strongly about their few remaining clutter spots as those who were losing the battle. Sadly, you can't just point a finger at the world and blame *it* for the clutter piling up in your home. After all, it is your space. No one is forcing you, or the people you happen to live with, to fill it with all that stuff. Nor is there anyone forcing you to keep it all (excluding that relative who insists you hang on to so-and-so's hideous china set, but we'll get to that later in the chapter).

Words like "overwhelmed," "nightmare," and "guilty" are highly charged; they are capable of sapping anyone of a substantial amount of energy and joie de vivre. We're hugely in favor of ditching the guilt. Clutter simply accumulates. If you don't have systems in place to deal with it on a regular basis, then it's going to be a problem. So rather than lose sleep or precious energy and goodwill over it, we say, learn why it accumulates and find ways to stay on top of it, using shortcuts wherever you can.

WHAT IS CLUTTERTOSIS, ANYWAY?

Cluttertosis occurs when you have an accumulation of clutter. We define clutter as anything that takes up space, physical or virtual, that either doesn't work or isn't making your life better on an ongoing basis. We admit that's a pretty broad definition. But we feel that getting any more precise than that is problematic. Why? Because choosing what to label clutter is a very personal decision; as the old saying goes, one man's trash is another man's treasure. To one, a collection of baseball cards is clutter. To that person's husband, it's anything but. For simplicity's sake, anything that (a) you don't really love, (b) you don't really need or use, (c) doesn't represent you or make you happy, or (d) doesn't work, is clutter.

WHY DOES CLUTTER ACCUMULATE?

Psychologists and professional organizers have a lot in common. In fact, when it comes to helping people eliminate clutter, it could be argued that professional organizers are functioning as psychologists. Why? Because so many of the reasons we cling to clutter tend to be emotional. Nancy Meyer, a vibrant sixty-year-old woman, found this out the hard way recently when she had to help her eighty-five-year-old mother make the transition to an assisted living facility.

"Going through her home and dealing with all of the clutter was a brutal process," she admits. "We battled over every little thing that I wanted to throw out or give away. You name it, she wanted to hold on to it: figurines I know she didn't really care all that much about, recipes she had torn out from various magazines and stored haphazardly in a drawer—some going back to the 1950s—a hideous serving bowl that she had received as a wedding gift (and that I never in my life saw used), and literally hundreds of other bric-a-brac. I really underestimated the emotional attachment factor. Sometimes the attachment was due to a fond memory, which I understood. But often the attachment was to something I knew she had never really used. It didn't make a whole lot of sense to me until I read somewhere that unused things often symbolize never-tapped potential to older people. To her, they were articles that represented a life she could have lived, things she could have done, but never got around to."

Nancy's revelation about her mom's pack rat ways applies to the rest of us as well. The primary reason anyone holds on to clutter is because they are emotionally attached.

- You have a fond memory associated with an item. Whether it's a piece of child's clothing, a ticket stub, a book, or an old high school paper, you hold on to it because you fear that if you let it go, the memory will be lost. The physical object is necessary to honor the memory.
- You received an item as a gift or an inheritance and don't want to offend the giver by getting rid of it.
- You fear you might need it someday.
- You fear it might become valuable someday.
- You are afraid to let the money you spent on an object go to waste.

The other reason clutter accumulates? Because it is so easy to overestimate the amount of time it will take to deal with it. As a result, we put it off and it really does become a problem. When you ignore it, clutter will pile up and pile up until dealing with it *does* become a major project, requiring lots of time and effort.

A FOUR-STEP CURE FOR CLUTTERTOSIS

As we said earlier, we strongly recommend losing any guilt or anxiety you have about your clutter. You're not a failure if you have it; we all do to some extent. No amount of wailing or gnashing your teeth is going to make it disappear as a problem. Happily, there are some straightforward ways to tame it. Simply use the four R's to guide you:

- *Routines:* Once established, simple routines take almost zero extra effort and are incredibly effective at keeping clutter at bay.
- *Rules:* Basic rules about when and how to deal with clutter eliminate the need to think too hard about what stays or goes; cleanup becomes automatic.
- *Regards:* Regarding your things through another's eyes (real or imagined) can be a helpful way to identify what is clutter so you can deal with it.
- *Reviews:* If you can't bring yourself to get rid of something, putting it in a review box for a specified period of time can make it much easier to part with once the allotted time is up.

ROUTINES

Clutter is a fact of life, so put in place a few routines to help you deal with the worst culprits of clutter in your house and reduce your headache. We peeked inside lots of people's homes during the past year, and by far the ones with the best handle on clutter were those who had established daily or biweekly routines for staying on top of the mess. Interestingly, they weren't obsessive or overly neurotic about getting every last bit of clutter. They prioritized which types of clutter to police and focused their routines on the ones that were most important to them.

Ann Smith, a divorced mom with two children who juggles a job *and* graduate school, has a million excuses to let the clutter piles accumulate. But she likes to have the visible parts of her house clutter-free, especially the bathrooms and the kitchen. "I like knowing that if someone were to walk through my house on any day, it's generally clutter-free. Of course, there are things I've made a priority, and those are the things that become part of my declutter routine. When I do little bits on a very regular basis, I do well. If I am confronted by a huge task, I'm very unlikely to do it because at the end of the day I only have so much energy. There are two places that must be clean at all times: the bathroom and the kitchen. I keep a sponge in the bathroom under the sink that I use to wipe down the bathroom vanity every night before I go to bed and every morning before I leave the house. I don't use a cleaner, I just wipe it down. You'd be surprised at how neat and clean that will keep your vanity. Nothing accumulates. You will never walk into my house and find hair or toothpaste in the sink. And I don't ever have to have giant bathroom cleans because that little bit every day does it. Once in a while, maybe every few weeks, I'll spray a little cleaning product, but generally, it's just water and a sponge. I love that I never have an 'Oh God, I have to clean the bathroom today' moment. The great thing about my routines is that they don't take up a whole lot of brain space. I use my 'routine times' to catch up with family and friends. If you ever talk to me on the phone, I'm doing something else at the same time that doesn't require thought, like putting dishes in the dishwasher."

Kerry Lyons, a mom to five under five, who also has a full-time job, uses her weeknight routine to help her stay on top of the inevitable clutter that accumulates with a big, busy family. It also helps her make it through the mornings. She explains, "I start out upstairs. I lay out clothes for my two older children, Liam and Ciara. Then I set up baby bottles for the triplets' night feedings. Then I move downstairs. I get the coffeemaker ready for the morning. I make sure the kitchen counter is scrubbed and the kitchen is clean. I make sure the paperwork is in neat and discreet piles. I check to see if the placemats and candles are straightened out and the chairs arranged neatly under the kitchen table. And then I do a quick tour to make sure all the toy trucks are in their parking lots, the dolls are in their chairs, etc. It takes all of ten minutes to do all of these things, but I swear it saves me half an hour of chaos and stress in the morning."

Jamie Osiecki, who produces a morning show in Philadelphia, also uses routines to keep clutter to a minimum and make her mornings hassle-free. "I scan around the house and I know what needs to be done to stay one step ahead of the clutter. If I take care of things the night before, it takes two and a half minutes, whereas it'll take me at least fifteen minutes to do the same thing in the morning. I can switch on the autopilot at night, which is what makes me faster, I think. The added benefit of doing a quick scan every night is that by doing it, I'll happen to look at something, like an electrical outlet, that will remind me to take care of something else, such as plug in a cell phone or computer to charge."

RULES

A handful of the women we spoke to had rules about either how much clutter they would tolerate before dealing with it or about what had to go out for something else to come into the house. Just as routines enable you to function on autopilot, rules provide clear guidelines for action that require little or no thought on your part. Once you have established a rule or two for either preventing clutter accumulation or dealing with it, abiding by the rule becomes a mere reflex.

Roxanne Lott has a rule that no junk mail will make it from her mailbox outside to the inside of her house. "Every night, when I pick up the mail from the mailbox, I swing by the garbage pail outside and dump anything that is junk. That includes catalogs. It keeps my mail pile headaches to a minimum."

Lori Wilson, journalist and co-host of Philadelphia's NBC *The 10! Show,* has a rule that she must deal with any lingering clutter before she leaves on a business trip. She says, "I don't have any nightly or even weekly routines. I tend to be a little bit more of a yo-yo organizer when it comes to clutter. I don't pick up every day. I'm going to live with a few pairs of shoes on the floor before I put them back on the rack, and like my mother, I'll go to bed with books on the bed. But I do travel a lot for work, and my rule is: I just can't come home to clutter. I need to clean it up before I can pack my suitcase and head out on a trip. It's just the way it is. So that's what helps me stay somewhat on top of the mess."

Angela Harris has a rule about what things make it beyond her mudroom. "I have a staging area in my laundry room. I have a rule that anything either I or someone in my family tends to take outside the house on a regular basis, like my purse, or the keys, or gym bags, must stay in there and cannot wander around the house. Having that rule means that we're all much more likely to know exactly where something is—no running around like chickens with our heads cut off at the eleventh hour looking for something—and it keeps clutter contained. It's not pristine, but it's contained in one area, which really works." Angela also has a rule about homework supplies, which can get messy and out of hand. "Everything the kids need to do their homework—pencils, tape, glue, markers, a dictionary, staplers, pencil sharpeners, a calculator, and paper—are kept in a cabinet in the kitchen. It's not at all pretty and organized, but it's contained in one place. They do their homework at the kitchen table or at the bar in the kitchen and everything they need is right there. It's also super easy to clean up."

A Pretty Neat Tip

MAKE A GAME OF IT

Even if you're not the most creative type, there are simple ways to make basic cleanup fun. More than a few women we interviewed routinely played games with their family to clear the clutter.

Gina Ward, a working mom with children ages eight, ten, and twelve, plays the ping-pong game mentioned in Chapter 5.

"Every other week or so, I'll take a bowl and fill it with ping-pong balls. Each ball has a task written on it with a Sharpie. Then I set the egg timer for fifteen minutes. The kids and I have to take a ping-pong ball and then race around the house picking up and putting away whatever is written on the ball. When you're done with one task, you come back and grab another ball. Whoever has the most ping-pong balls accumulated (besides me) at the end of the fifteen minutes gets a prize." Kathleen Ferguson and her family play a similar game before heading to church on Sunday mornings.

"We play the ten-pickup rule. I ask everybody to pick up ten things. 'Everybody, right now—put away ten things as fast as you can!' The one who does the best job putting ten things away the fastest gets a little treat. It makes a huge difference."

Michelle Bauman, on the other hand, uses a little rhythm to get her family in gear.

"We set aside twenty minutes of family cleanup time once a week. We crank up the music and make it fun. It's great because we know we have to clean, but now no one dreads the process."

Turning cleanup time into playtime isn't just good for the room, it's good for the family.

REGARDS

Taking a moment to regard the things you have through another's eyes is also a useful technique for tackling clutter. This is particularly true when it comes to tackling big clutter piles that have accumulated over time. A fresh perspective can help you drop your defenses and let go of things you've become attached to but no longer really need or use.

Sarah and Gardiner Welch take turns being the other person's clutter police. Sarah has a tendency to hold on to clothes and papers. Gardiner has a tendency to hold on to clothes and tech gadgets. Once or twice a year, when they do a significant purge, each one will serve as the judge and jury when it comes to determining whether the other person's stuff is clutter or not. Sarah explains, "Closets are a really tough thing for us to clean on our own because we both have a tendency to think, 'Oh I'll wear that again.' So I stand next to Gar when he's going through his clothes and ask questions like: Is it really flattering? When was the last time you wore it? Does it really fit your lifestyle now? If there are things he's waffling about, I'll cast the deciding vote about whether it stays or goes. If he is worried about how much he spent on what he's now giving away, I'll listen and suggest ways we could be thriftier in the year ahead. He does the same for me—especially when it comes to shoes. We have a similar problem when it comes to our home office. Every few months, we'll block off an hour or two on a week-night and tackle the clutter together. He keeps me honest as I go through my piles, and I keep him honest as he clings to techno gadgets that no longer work or he no longer uses."

REVIEWS

Another great tactic for dealing with significant clutter problems that have built up over time is a "review." Simply put, a review is a baby step in removing clutter that you're so attached to you can't bring yourself to get rid of it in the moment. During a review, you place items you think are no longer useful or needed in a temporary holding bin. If you find that after a specified amount of time you have not looked at or used any of the items in the temporary holding bin, get rid of the items—either by donating them or tossing them. For example, if you have a closet bursting with clothes but are unable to purge much of anything, take items you haven't worn in the past year and exile them to the basement or attic. If six months go by and you haven't worn a banished item, off to Goodwill it goes.

THE WORST CLUTTER CULPRITS

Clutter comes in various forms, some of it obvious, and some of it not. The physical clutter is easy to spot. Some of the worst culprits of physical clutter are mail, clothes, kitchen items, papers in the home office, virtual files, and toys (in fact, toys are such a problem that we've dedicated an entire chapter to them—see Chapter 9).

MAIL

Come rain, sleet, hail, or snow, the mail's delivered every day but Sunday. That means that every day you have a mixture of important (bills) and unimportant (junk) items making their way into your home that you have to deal with. According to Forest Ethics, a nonprofit dedicated to the eradication of junk mail, every household in America receives *more than eight hundred pieces* of junk mail each year and spends upwards of *eight months of their life* dealing with it![2]

The incoming mail spawns paper clutter for two reasons: (1) it tends to get dumped in a drop spot, like a kitchen counter, until you can deal with it, and (2) once you've sorted through the junk and opened the important items, some papers need to stick around until you've followed through with them, like paying a bill or putting an event on your calendar.

Simple Solution: Set up a mail station in a place that is steps from your main entryway. Be sure to put a stylish trashcan next to or underneath the station. As soon as you walk in with the mail, throw away the junk. Once a week empty that can into the recycling bin. Use a box or basket to hold the remaining mail. If you're inspired, get a multipronged sorter with three bins and label them: "pay me," "read me," and "respond to me."

CLOTHES

They do more than just keep us covered; they help us express who we are. It's so easy to go overboard on clothes, especially when tempting sales abound. Filling a closet is a whole lot easier than emptying it. But when it comes right down to it, the 80/20 rule truly applies to the clothes in your closet, in your drawers, in the hamper . . . and in storage. You really only wear a small percentage of the clothes that you have.

Clutter accumulates in your closet for a few reasons. For one, our need for variety keeps us constantly on the lookout for the new and nifty (just ask any pregnant woman who has had to wear the same darn clothes for nine months what a luxury variety is!). Fluctuating waistlines, happy memories, and sentimentality also keep us holding on to items longer than we should.

Simple Solution: Place a large cloth bag or two on the floor of your closet. Each day as you stare at your wardrobe, ask yourself three questions about one piece of clothing, a pair of shoes, and an accessory: (1) Is it flattering? (2) Do I love it? (3) Does it represent who I am today? If the answer to any one of these questions is no, put the item in the cloth bag straight away. Don't rationalize. When the bag is full, take it to Goodwill. Repeat as necessary until your closet only contains clothes, shoes, and accessories that you truly love and wear.

KITCHEN ITEMS

As the central gathering place for the family, kitchens are clutter magnets. The types of items that pile up are endless: food items, plastic containers, sports bottles (especially after sports games), cookbooks, children's backpacks, arts and crafts items, takeout menus . . .

There are many reasons clutter accumulates in kitchens. Jam-packed schedules and chaotic lives make it difficult to plan meals effectively, which means you're likely to have more food items than you really will need or use. Additionally, the central location (physically or emotionally) of the kitchen makes it the most trafficked room in the house, and therefore a natural dumping ground for bags, keys, toys, packages, and other random items. In the hustle and bustle, you don't ever take the time to declutter items that naturally accumulate over time.

Simple Solutions: Minimize food clutter by using step storage-risers and lazy Susans for your pantry. Then organize items so you can see what you have at a glance and access things easily. Mark expiration dates on perishable items with a marker and put older items in front of new items so you use them up first. Once you've reduced the clutter, always check your cupboards to see if you're out of something before adding it to your shopping list.

Establish clear zones for items like backpacks, purses, keys, and gym bags. If your space is big enough, put up a mirror with key hooks and a bench with baskets or bins underneath it. Designate that as the drop spot for all on-the-go items (if you have a mudroom, consider making this the one-drop stop instead).

Make two coffee dates with a friend. On the first coffee date, go to her house and help her go through her kitchen cabinets and identify and toss the clutter. On the second one, have her come to your house and reciprocate. Common culprits include chipped glasses, Tupperware, one-use aluminum bakeware that's crinkled and used, plastic cups, stirring utensils and spatulas, and pots.

PAPER FILES

We've all got them, those confounding stacks of receipts, catalogs, bills, and magazines that seem to appear out of nowhere and multiply the moment we leave the room. For most of us, they're part of the decor, a roving set of paper sculptures that attach themselves to any available flat surface in the house. We actually coined a term for this particularly annoying kind of clutter: *craplets*. Simply defined, a craplet is a piece of paper deemed too insignificant to command immediate attention, but too important to toss—like that *Men's Health* lying around that has the great ab workout in the back.

The main reason papers accumulate is because we're afraid we may need them again someday, but we don't have a straightforward filing system at the ready. For instance, it's possible you'll need to find the job receipt for the brand new roof that you put on your house three years ago. So, better safe than sorry, right? That may be true for some items, like documents related to home improvements, but you certainly don't need to hold on to sales receipts for minor purchases after you've satisfactorily used the item and it has no warranty.

Simple Solution: If you do nothing else, separating the things that require action from those that are simply for "safekeeping" will cut your headache in half. Have a durable, portable folder or plastic sleeve for those items requiring action and a sturdy inbox that will hold those items you need to file away for safekeeping. When you can, set up a system, whether it's with hanging files or accordion files, with twelve folders and label them as follows: medical, dental, legal, credit card statements, bank statements, insurance, taxes, home improvements, school papers, family documents. Leave two blank for miscellaneous files. Commit to filing for six minutes each day (two at the start of the day, two at lunch and two at the end of the day). You'll be pleasantly surprised at how quickly those piles disappear. In addition, take the action-item folder with you wherever you go and whittle away at its contents when you have time throughout the week.

VIRTUAL FILES

Who says clutter is a problem reserved for physical spaces like the hallway closet or your work desk? Although it's not as physically imposing as actual clutter, virtual clutter can wreak havoc on your ability to get things done. Whether it's the documents that pile up on your desktop or the emails that date back to the last decade, digital clutter makes it harder to interact with the basic functionality of your computer or device, or worse, slows it down dramatically.

The question of where to start is often the root cause of hesitation and procrastination. This is particularly true for virtual clutter, where the concept of cleaning up your files pertains to the desktop, your inbox, and potentially hundreds of other files. Considering that task monolithically is daunting to say the least.

Simple Solution: Focus your attention and energy on one specific area of your computer. Whether it's finally deleting or archiving those old emails or getting the multitude of your media downloads in one folder, pick one area

Meet: Kim Yorio

Family: Divorced mom with one son

Occupation: Public relations executive

Q: What amount of clutter is acceptable?

A: I generally can't stand clutter, so I try to stay on top of it as much as humanly possible. If I go over to someone's house who is a saver or hoarder, it tends to make me pretty anxious. So I guess I'd have to say, a very small amount of clutter is acceptable. That said, as long as it's behind closed doors (mine or someone else's), where I can't see it, I don't really care.

Q: What's the worst clutter culprit in your home?

A: The worst culprit for me is the mail. Having a mail station that is truly functional is my never-ending quest for the Holy Grail. I don't really have a place in my apartment yet for mail and it causes me great anxiety.

Q: What are your most effective tricks for dealing with the clutter?

A: My son and I play the moving game when we're trying to get rid of clutter. The great thing about moving is that it forces you to purge things because there's a real cost to moving something. So we just ask ourselves, "If we were to move tomorrow, would we pay to move this?" If the answer is no, we get rid of it. We try not to throw things away but rather sell or give them away to people we know need them.

Q: What are the triggers for actually wanting to tackle the clutter?

A: My great and shining moments of tackling clutter are always right before a business trip or a vacation. I'm a milestone-driven person, and going away really gives me a reason to get everything together.

and get started. You'll find that once you make some progress on one front, it's much easier to keep going. Commit to routine, bite-size checkups. Try taking five minutes to delete old emails and files while on your lunch break during commercial TV breaks, or after the kids are asleep.

CHAPTER WRAP-UP

Clutter is a major stressor. Rather than beat yourself up over it, we strongly recommend losing the guilt and anxiety that surround it. You're not a failure if you have it; we all do to some extent. No amount of wailing or gnashing your teeth is going to make it disappear as a problem. Simply use the four R's to tame it.

- *Routines:* Putting in place a few routines to help you deal with the worst culprits of clutter in your house will reduce your headache. Establish daily or biweekly routines for staying on top of the mess. Your routines shouldn't be obsessive or make you overly neurotic about getting every last bit of clutter. Instead, prioritize which types of clutter to police, and get in the daily or weekly habit of dealing with those in small windows of time.

- *Rules:* Establish rules about either how much clutter you will tolerate before dealing with it, or what has to go out for something else to come into the house. Just as routines enable you to function on autopilot, rules provide clear guidelines for action that require little or no thought on your part. Once you have established a rule or two for either preventing clutter accumulation or dealing with it, abiding by the rule becomes a reflex.

- *Regards:* When you have a major clutter pile to tackle, take a moment to regard the things you have through another's eyes. A fresh perspective can help you drop your defenses and let go of things you've become attached to but no longer really need or use. See it for what it really is.

- *Reviews:* If you're having trouble getting rid of things, take a baby step and put items in "review." Place items you think are no longer useful or needed in a temporary holding bin. If you find that after a specified amount of time, you have not looked at or used any of the items in the temporary holding bin, get rid of the items—either by donating or tossing them.

---

1. Storage Consumer Survey, *Homeworld Business Magazine,* October 1, 2008, www.homeworldbusiness.com/hw/main.asp.

2. "Climate Change Enclosed! Junk Mail's Impact on Global Warming." August 5, 2008, www.donotmail.org/section.php?id=3.

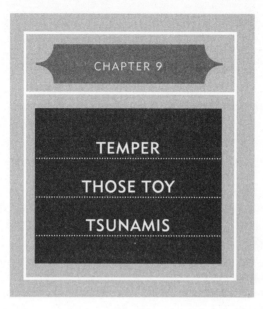

CHAPTER 9

TEMPER
THOSE TOY
TSUNAMIS

"The most effective kind of education is that a child

should play amongst lovely things."

—PLATO

It starts out slowly: a rattle here, a play mat there. But my, how quickly it escalates. Within one or two years of the arrival of your firstborn child, your home will have been hit by an inevitable toy tsunami. It's hard to say no to shiny, sparkly new items, and that's especially true when you can rationalize them as critical tools for helping little ones grow and develop. So in they stream. According to one study, the average American resident spends approximately $470 *per child* on toys, games, hobbies, tricycles, and battery-powered riders each year.[1] When you consider all of the people in your child's life (or children's lives), it's a miracle there is any room left in your house for furniture! Compounding the problem is the garish nature of many toys. It seems the more plastic and brightly colored the toys, the more that children like them. Their conspicuous nature only magnifies the issue; unless you're living in a multicolored plastic bubble full of geometric shapes and shiny surfaces, your children's toys will stick out like a sore thumb.

Rachael Petru-Horowitz's home is a case in point. She's a new mom and a neat freak who put her fundraising career on pause to stay home with her daughter, Polly. "When Polly was born, I naively thought we could contain all the toys and baby gear, so we set up a little play space for her in the living room with a big colorful mat and toy bins and everything. Fast-forward to our first big baby purchase: a swing that Polly just loved. Unfortunately, it had such a big base it took up the entire mat, which in turn meant everything else had to expand outward to accommodate it. In fact, Polly's outward expansion of toys was so rapid, her play space pretty much took over the entire house before she was even mobile. Our place went from serene and tidy to kid-clutter central. As a naturally neat person, it pains me to admit that I don't think it's possible to contain the clutter anymore."

TOYS, TOYS EVERYWHERE

Rachael's toy conundrum is typical. Children's clutter spreads like wildfire. Fellow first-time parents Sarah and Evan Sagal discovered just how fast it accumulates soon after they brought their son, Lev, home from the hospital. Sarah explains, "It's like our place went from zero to sixty on the clutter scale in just a couple of weeks. Our apartment was always bright and spacious, and we're both super organized. But then, I swear, it's like Lev's stuff started multiplying when no one was looking. He's this tiny person, yet his stuff is literally everywhere. Our home is starting to look like a daycare center, although this daycare wouldn't have much room for kids to actually play. We used to be proudly clutter-free, but we just haven't figured out how to manage all of his stuff."

Add more children to the equation and you've got a bigger problem. Cherell Jordan explains, "Our friends are in awe of how we manage such busy schedules, but my organizational Achilles' heel is the kids' toys. They're everywhere: the family room, bedroom, kitchen, you name it. When our kids want to find something specific, we don't even know where to start—it literally could be anywhere. So everything comes out while they search. Total disaster." Even parents lucky enough to have a basement playroom aren't immune. Just ask Liz Gruszkieviz, mom to three beautiful girls. "We are lucky to have a finished basement, which functions as the girls' playroom and a home office for me. We keep all of their toys down there in semi-organized bins, along with arts and crafts items, like crayons, paints, and easels. If it gets a little messy, we don't sweat it too much since it's downstairs and out of sight for visitors. That said, they certainly don't limit their playtime or toys to just that one area, no matter how much they love it down there! Every two or three days enough of their toys have migrated upstairs to the family room or to their bedrooms that you'd never guess we had a designated play area in the basement. It's a constant battle."

The fact is: kids are messy. They learn by diving into their things and putting them to the test. Mercifully, there are ways to stay a few steps ahead of chaos without depriving your kids of playthings.

GET SCHOOLED IN CLUTTER CONTAINMENT

Have you ever wondered why your child is a superstar during cleanup time at school, yet you struggle to get her to lift a finger at home? Schoolteachers have managing children's clutter down to a science, and we can learn a lot from them when it comes to keeping it all in check. Three simple rules keep school classrooms under control and maximize student participation:

1. Give everything a place.
2. Limit the number of items in circulation.
3. Set high expectations for participation and make it fun.

The same three strategies that work so well at school can also help you keep the toy clutter contained at home.

GIVE EVERYTHING A PLACE

It sounds so obvious, but you'd be surprised at how often this little thing is overlooked. Your kids cannot put their things away if they don't have a place to go. Looking around your house at the sheer volume of stuff, you may wonder if it is even possible to contain it all without spending a small fortune on storage bins. But there are lots of creative ways to contain toys and other kid clutter.

Gina's One Room Rule

When her three children's clutter got to be too much, Gina Bernstein came up with a straightforward solution: keep all the toys in one room—her youngest child's bedroom. Gina explains, "I'm an organized type, so I fully intended to keep the toys from taking over every room, but it's the kids' house, too, so the toys just spread. Then it started to get frustrating because pieces of things were scattered all over the place. Good luck trying to finish a puzzle or play a game; you'd find random pieces in every single room. Our solution was to keep all of the toys in only one bedroom, and to keep them visible so the kids can see them, not stuff them in a toy box. My daughter's room has lots of shelves, so we could easily put everything out and on display. At first, my kids had to adjust to keeping the shelves in order and to not having their own stuff, but it's all community property, and that's an important lesson in sharing. Containing the kid stuff has worked out really well for us."

Chris's Arts and Crafts Storage Boxes

Christine Smith engages the help of her son, Matthew, and twins, Grace and Allie, in creating and maintaining effective storage boxes for toys. "Each September, we create a new set of toy boxes for our playroom. Each child designs his or her own toy storage box as part of an arts and crafts day. First, I go to a store like Staples and buy some large, sturdy cardboard boxes. Then, back at home, we raid our craft supplies—looking for things like markers, paints, wrapping paper scraps, and stencils. On a spread of old newspapers Matt, Allie, and Grace each go to town decorating their own box (or two), putting bits of flair, pictures, and labels on them that they'll be proud to look at and use throughout the year. When they are done and the artwork is dry, we install them in the playroom as toy boxes for dolls, stuffed animals, trucks, and action figures. It's cheap, cheerful, and, most important, effective because they're invested in the solution."

Libby's Pegs

Make-believe is an integral part of childhood, and so are make-believe costumes. Libby Samuelson, mom of three girls between the ages of one and six, was up to her ears in princess dresses, veils, and pirate hats. She says, "I tried keeping them in a box, but the costumes spent more time out of it than in, and the girls never seemed to put them back when they were done wearing them. After a bit of contemplation, I realized that these costumes were more like overcoats than clothes. So I took a cue from my oldest daughter's classroom and mounted a series of hooks on their playroom and bedroom walls that made it easy for the girls to grab the costume they wanted and put it away when done. It's worked really well."

A Pretty Neat Tip

HOW TO ORGANIZE A TOY SWAP

When your kids start to get sick of their same old toys, it's time to plan a toy swap. The steps are simple, and the benefits—saving money, sharing with others, and all those new-to-you toys—are well worth the effort. Here's how to plan a toy swap.

1. Spread the word. Let families with children the same age as yours know about your event.

2. Set some ground rules. Write down the way you would like the swap to run. Will it be a one-to-one trade or will items be divided by their value? You might also consider letting the kids deal in a "currency" such as tickets or tokens.

3. Gather the goods. Collect items a day ahead of time so they can be ready to go on the big day. Arrange them by category so it's easier to browse.

4. Swap!

5. Donate. Choose a local charity, and arrange for them to pick up the remaining toys as soon as the swap ends.

There are alternatives to a person-to-person toy swap, such as local consignment shops and a few toy-swapping websites. We recommend:

• ToySwap.com

Susie's Baskets

As you set up your toy-storage systems, keep the future in mind. Your children will outgrow certain toys and want different ones at a rapid clip. Susie Feldstein, a mom to three, knows that toy storage must be flexible enough to meet your changing needs. "As a rule, little children have big toys, but as they get older their toys get smaller and have more intricate components . . . and a lot more pieces. My solution is simple: baskets, baskets, baskets! I've had them for years and years, and they're big enough to contain the toys. They look great because you can't tell if they're flawlessly organized— which they're most definitely not."

Once you've decided on an approach, work with your children to set up the system. Encourage them to classify their own stuff and figure out how to label the boxes. Let them pick silly names, anything to make it fun, and decorate the labels or containers as they like. The more involved they are in the process of defining the structure, the more invested they will be in the process of staying organized. Another added benefit of getting your children involved in structuring the approach: You're giving them much needed practice in an important life lesson, namely *how* to be organized. The more they practice classifying, organizing, labeling, and putting their things away, the better they will get at it. That skill will help them in their academic life and in their extracurricular life, and—here's the real bonus—it will help you keep a neater home with less effort!

LIMIT THE NUMBER OF ITEMS IN CIRCULATION

It's hard to put away toys when there isn't enough room for them. If your children have more toys than their toy box can hold, it's time to get rid of something. That might mean literally culling the number of toys your children have out at any one time, donating some to charity, or throwing out broken and unusable toys. Or it might mean reducing the number of toys in active rotation at any one time.

Denny's Giveaway Bins

When Denny Ticker's girls were young, she realized that if new toys were going to keep coming in, and they inevitably would, then she had to find a way to move out the old toys. She stuck a small bin she nicknamed "the giveaway bin" in the playroom and taught her kids to do the sorting for themselves. "I used to just wait until the toy box was overflowing, and then I'd go through it after the kids were in bed. I'd sneak out the toys that I thought they'd outgrown and off to Goodwill they'd go. Inevitably, I'd choose the wrong toy, and all hell would break loose. Can you imagine the pandemonium the day after I'd given something away when they realized that their favorite so-and-so was missing in action? Eventually, I wised up and put a small bin near the toy box, nicknamed the 'too little for me bin,' and when the kids came across a toy that they felt was too babyish for them, they'd put it in the giveaway bin. When it filled up after a few months, we'd go through it together. If they decided they weren't ready to part with a toy, then it stayed, but they also understood that everything in the bin was going off to another little kid who would love it just like they had."

Kate's Toy Rotation

Kate Mondloch, mom to seven-year-old Oliver, found herself battling toy creep from the time Oliver was two. She was eager to devise a system that stemmed the rising tide of toys that encroached on every room in the house. She explains, "From one day to the next it seemed as though two more toys had made it to the living room. So I instituted a toy rotation that cut his toys in circulation at any one time by a factor of three. Rather than keeping every toy out, I sat down one rainy Sunday and divided Oliver's toys into four mostly even piles. I was pretty careful to keep an interesting mix of toy types (e.g., stuffed animals, trucks, trains, blocks, and pretend play items) in each pile. My goal was to keep only one pile of toys out and in rotation at a time. When I was satisfied I had it roughly right, I put each set of toys in one or two extra-large Ziploc bags, and labeled it with a '1,' '2,' '3,' or '4.' Then I took all of the toys in bags labeled '1' and put them officially into rotation in Oliver's room—and I also put two or three toys out in the living room so that he had something to entertain him in there, but not too much. Every three months I rotate in the next bag of items, keeping the "out of rotation" toy bags in a closet where Oliver can't reach them." This technique has helped Kate and her husband reduce toy fatigue and makes toy-switching day a lot of fun as Oliver gets reacquainted with his "new" toys. "It's like Christmas every time we put the 'new' set of toys out."

A Pretty Neat Tip

TOY RECALLS

Every year, thousands of toys are recalled for being defective or dangerous. While you're sorting through the toy box, it's important to stay up to date on products that have been recalled. For information on toy recalls, Parents.com offers a user-friendly database at www.parents.com/product-recalls. Or visit the U.S. Consumer Products Safety Commission at www.cpsc.gov/cpscpub/prerel/prerel.tml.

Lauren's Annual Clean

When Lauren LaSalle's husband, Brian, slipped over a collection of wayward trucks on the stairs and broke his arm, they knew they had to do something to winnow the toys in circulation. They decided to have a Winter Cleanup party—and it was such a success that they now have it every year. "After Brian got hurt, we gathered our five boys and told them that they needed to identify toys that they thought they could do without. On a cold Monday night in January, everybody got together in the playroom and I set a kitchen timer to thirty minutes. There were three large boxes in the middle of the room: one labeled 'keep,' one labeled 'toss,' and the other labeled 'give away.' We instructed each of the kids to first identify and put in the toss box every toy that was broken and no longer functional. Once they did that, we got them to find at least ten toys or stuffed animals (that's fifty toys in total!) that were gently worn but no longer really useful, and put them in the give-away box. All other toys were put in the keep box. In one thirty-minute session, with the help of our motley crew, we reduced the number of toys around the house by at least a third!"

Christina's Scrapbook Solution

Sometimes your children aren't the ones with the hording problem! What happens if your little ones are ready to part with last year's favorite toy, but you're not quite ready to let it go? When Christina Harvell Brown's son, Griffin, was born she realized that her sentimental side was taking over. "All of the baby toys that Griffin loved dearly, even when he stopped caring about them, I just couldn't get rid of them. I knew I had to get it together and move them out or I'd be drowning in kid clutter pretty quickly. Now, for the things I am sentimental about, I take a picture and add them to a scrapbook of photos. Then I can get rid of the thing without parting with the happy memories. It really has worked for me."

SET HIGH EXPECTATIONS FOR PARTICIPATION AND MAKE CLEANUP FUN

Many parents who feel overwhelmed by the kid clutter also say that their kids are just too young to contribute more to cleaning up. Well, we disagree. If kids are old enough to toddle over and choose a toy, then they're old enough to put it away where it belongs when they are through playing with it. Children may not instinctively *want* to put their things away, especially if they are really excited about the next activity or a friend is over. But if you set the expectation that before moving on to the next activity they need to clean up what they just played with, then they will adapt over time. The trick to making it an ingrained habit is to start young, repeat the concept of "before we move on to the next thing, we have to clean up this," and model how toys should be put away.

Sarah's Lesson

Sarah Smith, mom to two toddler boys, is a convert to the idea that even two-year-olds can help with clutter. She explains, "Like most parents, we

A Pretty Neat Tip

GET ORGANIZED FOR TRAVELING WITH CHILDREN

Ensuring a happy and safe travel experience starts long before you leave the house. We recommend packing a backpack for each child that includes a few favorite toys, as well as one new toy. Starting at about age five, it's a great idea to get kids involved in the packing process. If you're traveling by plane, always bring snacks and a change of clothes, and keep the FAA's liquid limits in mind.

For infants:

• Pipe cleaners—twist one around each wrist and they will be fascinated, and if they are old enough, they will twist them on and off for at least a half-hour.

• Blue painter's tape—tear off a few pieces and stick them to the seat-back in front of you. They will entertain themselves for quite a while pulling the tape off and putting it back on the seat again and again. Just be sure to monitor your child as she's playing with the tape. You want her to play with it, not eat it!

For kids ages two to five:

• Coloring books with crayons
• Favorite books
• Magnetic stick-together blocks
• Play dough
• Portable DVD player

For kids ages five to nine:

• Books about your destination
• Playing cards
• Travel games with magnetic pieces and boards
• Portable electronics with headphones

had a tendency to coddle our firstborn. I figured that until he was at least three or four, he was just too little to put his own things away so I would always pick up after him. But by the time he started going to nursery school, at three, he was so used to having me pick up after him that he was genuinely confused when all of a sudden others, including me, wanted him to put

Meet: Ann Malone Smith

Family: Divorced with two children

Occupation: Administrative assistant

Q: How do you wrangle your children's toys?

A: I have a very unscientific method for containing their clutter: a humongous toy chest that we keep in their playroom. Everything can fit in there. Is it totally disorganized on the inside? Yes. But if they want something, they can find it with a little looking. I think the fact that it's not a complicated system makes it easier for the kids to use.

Q: What cleanup habits do you expect your kids to have?

A: Cleanup is just a part of our everyday routine; it's built into the daily schedule. The kids know that as soon as it is cleaned up, we'll do X. It's also built into our nightly routine of getting ready for bed. Every night before they put on their pj's, they clean up their rooms and their playroom. If I can see that things are messier than usual, I'll leave a little extra time for bed. They know it and don't fight it. It just becomes a habit. So I'd say I have high expectations. And I've found that they really do rise to meet those expectations.

Q: How involved are you in the cleanup routine?

A: One of the hardest things to do as a parent is to get your kids to do it themselves. I definitely feel strongly that if you don't do it for them, they'll learn to do it themselves. When it comes to cleaning up, I don't do any of it for them. I have tried to make it a part of the routine so that it becomes something you do once a day, not a big chore.

Q: What advice would you give to a parent who is having a hard time getting their kids to pick up their toys?

A: First I'd ask them what "pick up" means to them. Some parents get hung up on the idea of having color-coded boxes for different toys, etc., and expect their kids to put things away precisely. If that were the case, I'd recommend a simpler approach, like a giant toy box. Isn't the point just to have clutter off the floor and out of sight when toys aren't being used? If that wasn't the issue, but follow through was, I'd probably advise the parent to tie a consequence to not putting the toys away, like having toys left on the floor confiscated. You have to be super consistent with kids to get them in the habit of doing something, so make sure once you institute a rule, you follow through on it every day.

his own toys away. It took a lot of time, not to mention temper tantrums, for him to unlearn the dependency I created. Our second son was born around that time and we promised ourselves we would not make the same mistake. As soon as he was old enough to play with any real toys, I always made a point of saying out loud, 'We always have to put this away before we can get something else out,' and modeling how to put away the current toy. He's now two and a half and generally puts away his things without a fuss when he's done playing with them. Of course, he's a different child with a different temperament than my first, but I am convinced that simply having the expectation from the beginning that he should put away his toys on his own made a world of difference."

Eileen's Leeway

Expectations do help. So does a little flexibility. Eileen Opatut, a working mom with three teenagers, describes the benefit of having some wiggle room. "My kids know that certain spaces just have to stay neat. I'm okay with a little clutter in the kitchen and playroom—as long as it's cleaned up at the end of the day—but messes are never allowed in the living room. They do their best to keep those spaces in order, and we're all happier because of it."

Mara's Chart

Mara Goldstein, a physician and mom to three kids, implemented a responsibility board to get her kids involved in the decluttering process. "I believe that some kids are just born with the organizing gene. I was one of those kids, but my three are definitely not. A few years ago we instituted a responsibility board to try to get the kids to do their part. It includes: clearing plates, brushing teeth, making beds, putting clothes in laundry bin, and organizing toys. They get an allowance based on the board, and it has helped them get in the habit of taking care of their things much better." Like Eileen, Mara has also learned to check her perfectionist and control-freak tendencies at the door and let her kids organize their things in a way that makes sense to them. "My son inherited my collector's gene, and he loves comic book superheroes. Well, those toys are so important to him that he has his own way of arranging them—Justice League, Marvel, and more—and so he had to train me how to do it the 'right' way. I'm happy to follow his lead, because he's in charge of caring for his things."

CHAPTER WRAP-UP

Teaching your children how to get and keep their toys organized is an important life lesson that will pay dividends for them. Busy moms from all walks of life have shown us that there are creative and fun ways to ensure that their children develop good organizational habits. Although in the moment, kid clutter can seem impossible to tame, there are three simple steps to getting it all buttoned up.

- *Give Everything a Home:* It sounds so obvious, but it is absolutely essential. Your kids cannot put their things away if there is no place to put them. Encourage your children to put their own stamp on toy storage; the more they participate in designing the storage solutions, the more likely they are to use them.
- *Limit the Number of Items in Circulation:* It's hard to put away toys when there isn't enough room for them. If your children have more toys than their toy box can hold, it's time to get rid of something.
- *Have High Expectations and Make Participation Fun:* Expect them to be organized—don't throw up your hands and do it all for them. They'll never learn that way, and you'll always have more on your plate than you need to. Let go of the need to oversee every detail of what they are doing and the requirement that they get it done perfectly. Instead, establish fun, structured routines that instill good habits that can be put to use over a lifetime.

---

1. Brad Edmondson, and Berna Miller, "Who gets the toys? Do the best little girls and boys get the most toys on Christmas Day? Demographic aspects of Christmas toy buying," *American Demographics,* December 1997.

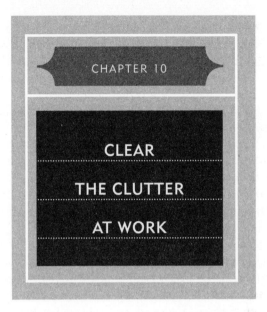

CHAPTER 10

CLEAR

THE CLUTTER

AT WORK

"If a cluttered desk is a sign of a cluttered mind,

then what is an empty desk a sign of?"

—ALBERT EINSTEIN

Marcy Gussin thinks she's got better things to do at work than get organized (and judging by the state of many offices we've seen, a big percentage of people feel the same way). Marcy works as a project manager for a major mortgage company and the issue for her is time. She admits, "Clutter makes me feel anxious and unproductive, so I try to tidy up a little here and there. But my office, especially my desk, is a disaster area and I just don't see any way around that. My company has downsized recently and as a result my workload is through the roof. I really can't rationalize taking hours out of my day to put it all in perfect working order. No way."

Marcy's right, right? After all, time spent organizing isn't billable. It doesn't really produce anything of measurable value. And it's not generally part of your job description. In fact, it is easy to conclude, just as Marcy has, that the time it takes to get organized only diminishes the time you have to take care of the really important stuff on your to-do list. But that's just plain wrong. Just because organization isn't an explicit part of your job doesn't mean you can do without it.

CAN CLUTTER GET YOU FIRED?

Clutter at work is a silent killer. It drains you of energy, saps productivity, and potentially costs you the esteem of colleagues and bosses. Psychological researchers have found that the constant barrage of clutter we face at work leads to higher levels of cardiovascular stress, impaired judgment, and a noticable drop in civility to others.[1] Stress, bad judgment, and crankiness— not high on the list of career-advancing traits, are they?

Why is clutter at work such a problem? For starters, it acts as a visual white noise that your eyes and brain have to process. The additional stimuli constantly distract you from the work you really need to do. And it's not like you can just close the door and pretend it doesn't exist. You spend roughly half of your waking hours working, so you're constantly reminded of your general state of disorganization and your lack of gumption in tackling it.

Clutter is a time suck, too. According to a recent survey by the National Association of Professional Organizers, people who are disorganized at work estimate that they waste between thirty minutes to an hour *each day* hunting for a lost document or something else they need.[2] That adds up to anywhere from between two-and-a-half to five hours in lost productivity each week. You can imagine how that number compounds over the course of a year. It translates into many weeks worth of lost productivity or overtime you have to invest to get the job done. That doesn't go unnoticed by superiors. According to a 2005 study comissioned by Sanford Brand's subsidiary DYMO, the cleanliness and organization of an employee's desk are considered by more than half of America's managers when they conduct annual reviews, hand out raises, and offer promotions.[3] And they look more positively at those who are buttoned up than they do at those who are slobs: 51 percent of the 2,600 bosses interviewed worldwide said they think there's a link between an employee's organizational skills and their job performance. The fact is, whether you've got an office, a cube, or a desk in a corner of the bedroom, if it's a cluttered, disorganized mess, you simply cannot do your best work there.

Maggie Riso, an administrative assistant at an Internet startup, sums it up perfectly. "Clutter sucks my will to work. I have a really intense boss who relies on me to be on top of every detail. When I have a lot of different things on my desk all clamoring for my attention, I feel overwhelmed and am easily distracted. I just know something important is going to get lost in the shuffle. The tension I feel spills over and makes me snappy and defensive when I have to deal with other people. On the other hand, when my desk's neat and organized, I get things done faster. It puts me in a good mood because I feel like I'm able to really contribute."

An absentminded, Nobel Peace Prize–winning professor may be able to pull off a messy work space, but most people just can't work in a cluttered environment without suffering the consequences. In the workplace, clutter comes at a high cost, whether you realize it or not.

IS CLUTTER MAKING YOUR DESK DIRTIER THAN A TOILET SEAT?

Clutter does more than just sap you of productivity and stress you out. It can also make you sick. Literally. NEC Mitsubishi, a maker of computer monitors, questioned two thousand office workers in the United Kingdom in 2005 and found many to be suffering from what they wryly coined "Irritable Desk Syndrome (IDS)." The effects of IDS are anything but funny. According to the study, IDS is caused by working long hours at a cluttered desk often with poor posture. The combination can lead to both physical and mental symptoms, including chronic pain and an inability to focus. Fully 40 percent of those surveyed said they were infuriated by the clutter on their desk but couldn't be bothered to do anything about it. Another 35 percent admitted they suffer from back or neck pain because they knowingly sit at their desk in an awkward position—working around the problem rather than simply dealing with it.[4] If you've got a coffee mug or a pin with a slogan like "a clean desk is a sign of a sick mind" or frequently claim to incredulous visitors that you know exactly where everything is in spite of the chaos, you might be intimately familiar with the symptoms of IDS.

If that isn't disturbing enough, a study done by the University of Arizona in 2002 found that the typical worker's desk has hundreds of times more bacteria per square inch than an office toilet seat. Four hundred times more to be exact. That's just plain gross! And the messier it is, the less likely it is to get cleaned. At most offices, custodians won't touch desks littered with stuff because they're afraid they'll accidentally misplace or lose something important. The moral of the story here: The messier your desk, the more at risk you are for catching the types of colds and infections that can put you out of commission.

EXCUSES, EXCUSES

Clearing the clutter at work is good for business. Not only does it make an excellent impression on clients and colleagues, but getting organized and staying organized helps you get things done faster, feel more fulfilled, and clears your mind for creative thinking and productivity. It's also good for your health. So why aren't we all motivated to keep our work spaces a little more buttoned up? It might have something to do with the stories we tell ourselves.

Adam Rockmore is a case in point. As a busy entertainment industry executive, he tells himself (and those near and dear to him) that he functions well amidst chaos. "I've got a messy desk, but I know exactly where things are and what I need to do. It's my own style, you could say. Besides it doesn't impact my work, so I deal with it." Really Adam? It *never* affects your work? "Well, every once in a while, I can't find stuff, and that's just unacceptable," he confesses. "When that happens, I tackle the piles for a few hours. I do a massive cleaning job, and the place definitely looks worse before it looks better. I guess I'm okay with clutter—except when I can't find stuff. That's no good for business, but it's not like my mess has cost me my career."

Megan Lipshultz, a hardworking personal assistant in Los Angeles, thinks she struggles with a messy desk because the stuff at work isn't really *hers*. At home, she owns the paperwork, but at work there's just not the same sense of ownership, which makes her feel less motivated to keep things organized. "It's this weird situation at work because I love my job, but it's really someone else's life that I'm running. That shows when I let stuff pile up around me. I'd never let that happen at home, but my boss isn't concerned, so I let it slide. That's fine until I need something that is lost somewhere in the shuffle. Whenever that happens, I'm reminded that it's not mine but it *is* my job!"

Leah Ticker, a first grade teacher, tells herself that she just doesn't have the time to get her desk organized. "I think teaching is all about learning—for me and the kids. After I teach a lesson, my goal is to make notes about what I can do better for next year and then file them away. I create portfolios for my students, too, so they can see all that they've accomplished. But it's not like I can tell twenty-one six-year-olds to entertain themselves while I take the time to arrange everything. Stuff just piles up higher and higher, so even if we might need something later, there's not much chance of finding it ever again."

Lindsay Roberts, an Atlanta-based law recruiter, blames communication overload for her organizational woes at work. "At the law firm, I work amidst an endless stream of instant messages, phone calls, meetings, and interviews that happen in real time, all the time. Then there are the emails, trade publications, and proposals that pile up while I'm busy doing my job. All of these modes of communication are great in theory, but the overload is keeping me from tackling the physical mess I've got on my hands."

Excuses, no matter how good and rational they sound, are simply roadblocks to a happier, more productive work environment. Most of us have bad days (or weeks) where stuff piles up because we're too busy to file papers, sort through the mail, throw out old sticky notes, or generally dig out from under the onslaught of work. But don't lull yourself into believing that you're just a messy-office type and that there's no hope for you. Everyone is capable of having a relatively buttoned up desk area. But where to start?

TRIGGER YOUR TIP-OFF POINT

Having a messy office is kind of like having a mosquito bite. If you're focused enough on something else, you can ignore your desire to scratch the itch for a little while. But the itch slowly gets worse and worse. If you try to resist scratching it, it just gets more annoying. Soon, it's all you can think about; it consumes you. Until finally, you can't stand it anymore, so you reach around and give that bite a good, long scratch. Ah, relief. You might call that moment where you cave in and scratch the itch a tipping point. It's a point at which it becomes more painful and annoying not to deal with something than to soldier on and try to ignore it.

Once you hit the tipping point for dealing with your office clutter, there is no turning back. The first step in transforming yourself from an office mess into an office model is figuring out how to trigger your tipping point. Take the quiz below to get the appropriate dose of office cleaning motivation to get you over the hump.

SHORTCUTS TO OFFICE SERENITY

Once you've triggered your tipping point, you need ways to stay on top of office disorder that take a minimum of time and energy: shortcuts to office serenity, so to speak. That's because, even though staying organized at work

TIPPING POINT QUIZ

1. I can see what percentage of my desktop:
   A. All of it. My desk is pretty clean and clear. (1 point)
   B. Less than half of it is visible. (3 points)
   C. Is there a desk under there somewhere? (5 points)

2. I would describe my clutter piles as:
   A. Categorized by topic and/or due date. (1 point)
   B. Not organized per se, but I am confident I can find what I need. (3 points)
   C. Just one big amorphous pile. I'm not really sure what's in there. (5 points)

3. I go through and sort and clear out my piles:
   A. At least once a week. (1 point)
   B. At least once a month. (3 points)
   C. Are you supposed to do that? (5 points)

4. If someone saw my work space, they might say:
   A. I could work at your desk. (1 point)
   B. It's ordered chaos, but I can see how it works for you. (3 points)
   C. When did the tornado hit? (5 points)

Less than 7 Points: You're naturally organized and tend to stay on top of the clutter. If you're lacking motivation today, just close your eyes for a minute before you leave work and really try to picture yourself walking into work tomorrow. Imagine how great you'll feel when you see a pristine desk. That should be all the motivation you need to take one or two additional minutes to tidy up before you head out.

is critically important, we all have more important things to do. Happily, plenty of busy business people we interviewed have found simple ways to restore order and efficiency to their offices. Their tricks generally fall into one of three categories: (1) basic routines for staying neat, (2) basic paper filing systems, and (3) basic electronic filing systems. Of course, their tips and tricks aren't perfect, but they get the job done well enough, and that's what really matters. Follow their lead to clear the clutter quickly and get back to work.

BASIC ROUTINES FOR STAYING NEAT

Clearing clutter at work is just like clearing it at home—you will always have to do your best to stay on top of it. Just as we recommend putting in place a few routines at home to help you deal with the worst culprits of clutter, the same holds true for the office. Those officemates of yours who

7 to 11 Points: You manage to clean up your clutter when you absolutely need to but are skilled in ignoring it. You're stuck in this cycle because you have a belief that you are not capable of being consistently buttoned up. It doesn't have to be that way! You can break the habit by rewiring your brain to associate getting organized with fun so that you always enjoy staying one step ahead of the mess. How, you ask? Establish a new habit. Take five minutes at the end of every day, blast the tunes on your computer, and at the very least, put the things on your desk in orderly piles. Start today—and as you walk out the door, take a look back at your neat(er) office and think of how good it feels to be able to get things generally in order without having to slave for hours. Do the same tomorrow and the next night, and then the next. Pretty soon, you'll be rewired.

Over 11 Points: You have a long way to go—and since that's the case, you're probably suffering from a severe case of organizational inertia. (That's just a fancy way of saying it will take a whole lot of effort to tackle the disaster area, and that's energy you just don't have to spare, so you'll just keep soldiering on as you were.) The most effective way to overcome organizational inertia is to just do something to change the state of things. Go download the *Rocky* theme song on iTunes if you don't already have it, press the repeat button on your computer's music player, and crank it. Then focus on one small area of your work space and give yourself fifteen to twenty minutes (roughly five to six rotations of the song) to clean it up. When you're done, revel in your Rocky moment. Look back at what you accomplished and celebrate how great it feels to have done it. Do the same thing tomorrow and each following day until you've tackled the mess. Of course, don't be surprised if you are so inspired by what you accomplished in your initial fifteen-minute cleanup that you carve out a massive block of time and tackle the chaos in one fell swoop.

manage to have clutter-free work spaces tend to have established regular routines for staying on top of the mess. They don't obsess about having the perfect filing system or an absolutely pristine desk. They simply focus on doing a few things consistently to keep their work space relatively under control. The most effective routines can be done on autopilot and squeezed into small windows of time.

Unfortunately, clearing the clutter at work is not a one-shot deal. Whether you establish a daily, weekly, or monthly routine for clearing the clutter is up to you. The key is that you do one or two things to organize the stuff in your office frequently enough that you avoid having to spend hours digging out from under. Here are a few simple routines that work.

Christine's Friday File

Christine Patrick, an office manager for a plumbing company, does her filing on Friday afternoons, an activity she calls "harvesting paper clips." She explains, "I file on Friday afternoons when I don't want to do anything else. Filing isn't my favorite task, but it is something that just has to get done. I usually have a pile of things that has been building up all week, and it feels good to get it off my desk into appropriate folders. I create new files once a month—so if something lingers in a miscellaneous file for a few weeks, I don't stress about it too much because I know it will find a home soon enough."

Jeff's Immediate Action Plan

The fact is, the more time you take thinking about paper clutter, the more the clutter collects. For Jeff Anderson, vice president of a technology company, the key to managing those workplace paper piles is quick decisions followed by immediate action. "I ask myself: Do I need this? If the answer's no, then it immediately gets tossed or shredded. If the answer's yes, it gets filed right then and there. If I don't make quick decisions—and follow through on them—then the piles sit there and, after a few weeks, it's out of control. For me, the best way to manage the mess is to be decisive."

Lexie's Tool Trimming

When Lexie Watson, a French translator for an international financial company, tackles a new task at work, she takes two minutes to remove anything on her desk not related to the task at hand. She doesn't obsess about where she puts things; she'll stash items in a drawer, holding bin, or temporary file folder if she doesn't have a lot of time. "It's important to keep the right things close at hand, but my desk space is at a premium, so for me it's just as important to clear the desk of the stuff I don't need. Any papers or piles that don't relate to what I'm doing right now are just going to distract me. I also include computer-related tools in my clear-the-desk routine, especially if I really need to focus. I'll close out my email program, hit the do-not-disturb button on my phone, and turn off my ringer on my cell so that my focus stays where it should be."

Lauren's Neat Notebook

A lot of paper clutter can be reduced by keeping an office notebook—a virtual notebook or a physical one. It can be the perfect place for keeping daily or weekly to-do lists, jotting down phone numbers, taking notes, and just generally staying on top of details. Lauren Hudson, a marketing assistant at an Internet company, relies on her virtual notebook to keep the clutter at bay. "It sounds like a no brainer, but my virtual notebook is my lifesaver. If I didn't use it my desk would be drowning in a sea of Post It Notes. Instead, I keep tasks and notes from phone conversations in a Microsoft Word document. The document has a few columns with general headings, and then I just use that to keep track of all the to-do's and notes associated with each area. Anytime it starts to get unweildy, I can start a new one. I've found it really helps me keep clutter to a minimum. You can also use a physical notebook to accomplish the same thing. You just have to remember to force yourself to look back at the notebook for the first few weeks until it becomes a habit."

Clutter piles spread like weeds when you have no containment strategy. Happily, all it takes to keep things under control is a simple routine. If you can take a few minutes to tame your desk on a regular basis, you'll never have to spend hours searching for things or digging out from under the clutter.

BASIC PAPER FILING SHORTCUTS

Elaborate filing systems are overrated. Yes, those pictures of color-coded files with impeccably printed labels shown off in glossy magazines and catalogs are truly works of art. If you had an entire day to devote each month to managing your files, you too could have a system like that. But that's not reality for the vast majority of workers. What really matters when it comes to wrangling papers effectively is that those papers and files that you need are easily accessible. In the end, an elaborate filing system may not be the most efficient thing anyway, since there is a point at which having additional folders makes it *more* difficult to put your hands on what you need when you need it. Simple systems are truly the most effective, whether you're a file person or a pile person. Here are some simple ones you might want to emulate.

Kim's Pile Files

Kim Davis has embraced a piling system to stay organized. "At work, I've got some piles here and there, but it's not a clutter problem. Those piles are my solution. I keep the piles growing throughout the week when I don't want to waste time filing stuff that I may not need later. Then, the key to managing my piles is a cup of coffee on Friday afternoon. It's kind of a Zen way to end the week by putting everything back in order. It definitely works for me." She elaborates, "If you tend to be a piler, not a filer, create a piling system that works for you. Think about how you look for a particular piece of paper, and then create two or three simple categories for piles. Don't stress if you don't get it right the first time. Sooner or later you will come up with a system that works for you. My piles are organized into three categories: urgent, to read, and follow-up. It doesn't have to be complicated to be effective!"

Lisa's Major Categories

Lisa Hale *hates* filing papers, but as a special education teacher, it comes with the territory. "I hate to file papers, so I've created a simple system that I use a majority of the time and about four times a year I conduct complete filing. Depending upon what I'm working on, I create file folders for what I call the major categories—there are about five at any one time. I buy decorative file folders because they make me feel better about filing. Then I perch them in an inclined file sorter behind my desk, where I can easily reach them. It's easier for me to dump my papers into a handful of major categories than it is to file them away with very specific labels. About four times a year, or once I have gathered too many papers under a major category, I sit down and go through them. At that time, I dump what is not needed any longer and organize the remaining papers into more specific files that I place in my filing cabinet."

Lauren's Tiered Files

Lauren Hudson keeps what she needs at her fingertips. "It would be great if I was able to keep all of my files in electronic format, but paper still has its place! I'm very prone to losing loose documents, so I like to keep them organized by topic in old-fashioned file folders—that way there is still some sort of method to the madness and I'm much less likely to lose something (and more likely to find it when I need it). I keep real top-of-mind/current projects stacked in a tiered file holder so I can literally keep an eye on everything I'm working on. I keep the tiers in order of urgency/relevance. The farther back the file, the less attention it needs. Once a folder has made its way up the tiers, it's eventually retired to a drawer where I can find it again if I need it."

The purpose of a filing system is so you have easy access to the stuff you need to do your job. The simpler and more straightforward it is, the more likely you will actually use it.

BASIC ELECTRONIC FILING SYSTEMS

Storing information electronically has plenty of advantages. Virtual files take up no physical space, are accessible from anywhere, and are easy to share with others. Plus they are secure (or at least more secure than that cabinet you never take the time to lock). If a document is important enough to keep, then maybe it could and should be stored electronically.

Sara Furie, a finance manager for a major newspaper, got on board with electronic filing when she could no longer keep up with the paper clutter. "My desk was always overrun with paper copies, and I lose paper copies in my disorganized file cabinet all the time. Electronically, I am organized. It's so easy to save everything in folders. I have gotten to the point that if someone gives me a paper copy, I PDF it and save it in my electronic files." Ryan Browne, an operations director at a technology company, agrees, saying, "I'm not a fan of paper files. If I had the time, I would scan everything I had and shred afterwards. As a result, I really keep a minimum amount of paper."

As with paper filing systems, the keys to a good electronic one are simplicity and manageability.

Jennifer's Filing by Format

Jennifer Kelly, a technical writer, keeps her office clutter-free by doing everything electronically. She also has a super-simple filing system that makes a whole lot of sense.

"When it comes to keeping electronic files straight, I've tried a lot of methods over the years and have landed on one that works for me. First I have a very small handful of master categories that I file things into (Current Workload, 2009 Completed Projects, 2008 Completed Projects, etc.). I file

Meet: Amy Corvino

Family: Single

Occupation: Medical sales representative

Q: Do you have any routines to help you stay on top of clutter?

A: Yes! As a sales rep, I collect a lot of business cards—at the end of the day, it's not uncommon for me to have amassed thirty of them. So I bought two soft binders and business card inserts. One binder is for New Jersey clients and the other is for New York clients. The laws are different for each state, therefore I like to keep them separate. I file cards in each binder by category/medical specialty. Also, I take notes throughout the day and at the end of the day or week (if I'm behind), I enter all the information into spreadsheets that are broken down by category/medical specialty. Then I print out the spreadsheets, and put them into the binders with the business cards. That system really helps me keep paper clutter to a minimum.

Q: Since you are on the road a lot, do you even keep paper files?

A: I do have a filing system, because I can't keep everything in the binders—they are really for making sure I keep things straight when I'm on the road. I have a filing cabinet in my home office that is organized into two colors. One for New Jersey and one for New York clients, just like my soft binders. The files are ordered alphabetically by the client's last name. I have mesh bins labeled "Follow Up" and "File Away" on my desk to collect wayward papers. I take care of everything in the Follow Up tray every day. But I'll only deal with the papers in the File Away bin once a week. Sometimes I need to refer to a paper that has to be filed away, so that's why I wait until the end of the week before filing things.

Q: What about electronic files?

A: I have a laptop with me all the time—so yes, I've got lots of electronic files. I break electronic files down by category. For example: expense reports, mileage log, etc. As soon as documents are opened or created, I save them immediately into the correct folder. I try to keep naming conventions really simple, so things like expense reports are saved as month and year. That way I can always find what I'm looking for.

Q: What advice would you give to someone who is struggling to stay on top of office clutter?

A: It sounds obvious, but having one or two small things that you do every day is going to have the biggest impact on your ability to keep your office organized. If I didn't have my two binders, I'd be buried in clutter and probably a lot less effective.

documents into sub-folders first by project name and then by document format (i.e., MS Word, MS Excel, MS PowerPoint), because for me, I may not remember the name of the file, but I remember what type of file it was. We use enough different file types for this to work for me. Eventually, completed project folders outlive their usefulness and are deleted. As projects are completed, I move the files from the current workload file to the appropriate folder—typically about once a month. If I can't find something quickly in these file folders, then I run a keyword search in Windows Explorer. Since I'm searching so few folders, the results usually pop up quickly."

Ryan's Desktop Shortcut

Ryan Browne works in a technology company and does his best to do everything electronically. To keep things he's working on easily accessible, he uses his computer desktop.

"I use my desktop for my scratchpad/work-in-progress files. I'll file them away into appropriate categorized folders when I'm finished with them. Sometimes my desktop gets overrun, and when that happens, maybe once every few weeks, I'll spend some time (twenty minutes tops) cleaning it out and putting files I no longer need to have at my fingertips in more specific folders."

Hollie's 1-2-3

As the design director for Buttoned Up, Hollie Sehrt could easily get overwhelmed by electronic files. To keep her files streamlined, she employs a simple three-step approach.

"When it comes to files, I have to be organized. Typically for each project I'm working on, I'll go through at least three or four different rounds of designs and tweaks before getting to a final file. If I'm not vigilant in eliminating drafts, I wouldn't be able to ever figure out which was the *final* final file, which is dangerous if you have to print one thousand pieces of something! So I instituted a simple three-step system that works for me. Step one: I keep a master list of folders that represent the constants of my work—for example, new products or marketing or website—and that master list really hasn't changed in two or three years. Step two: Within those big master folders, I have project folders, such as ebrochures or website illustrations that I add as new projects come up. I save all individual files to their appropriate project folder. Step three: When I save an individual file, I name it using the following convention: date_name of file_version#. That way, I can always easily find the most recent version of something. I make sure to get rid of old files or retire old folders that are no longer in use every three months. Most important, I set my computer to back everything up automatically each night."

We're all probably a little guilty of saving at least a few files to the desktop or random folders and letting them linger there a bit too long. But if you aren't careful, your computer can quickly become something we like to call the virtual dump. Don't be constantly frazzled because you can never remember what you named important documents or which files are current and which are old. To keep your computer free from this form of digital clutter, set in place a simple filing structure and stick to it.

CHAPTER WRAP-UP

Let's face it: Work is a busy, busy place. It can be tempting to think that you don't have the time or the need to keep your work space in order. Orderly offices enhance your productivity and creativity, while messy workplaces stress you out, waste your time, throw your judgment off, and make you a grump. Bottom line: Clean offices and work spaces are good for business.

The first step in transforming yourself from an office mess into an office model is figuring out how to trigger your tipping point. That simply means getting to a point at which it becomes more painful and annoying to not deal with your messy desk than to soldier on as you were. Once you're ready to face the demon, three things can help you keep it neat over the long haul:

- *Establish a Cleanup Routine:* Clearing the clutter at work is not a one-shot deal. Whether you establish a daily, weekly, or monthly routine for clearing the clutter is up to you. The key is to do one or two things to organize your office on a regular enough basis that you avoid having to spend hours digging out from under.
- *Keep Paper Filing Basic:* What matters most when it comes to wrangling papers effectively is that important papers and files are easily accessible. In the end, an elaborate filing system may not be efficient, since there is a point at which having additional folders makes it more difficult to put your hands on what you need when you need it. Simple systems are truly the most effective, whether you're a file person or a pile person.
- *Go Electronic:* Virtual files take up no physical space, are accessible from anywhere, and are easy to share with others. Plus they are secure.

Implement a simple folder setup and file-naming convention that makes it easy to find files.

---

1. P. Waddington, "Dying for Information? A report on the effects of information overload in the UK and worldwide," 1997, www.cni.org/regconfs/1997/ukoln-content/rep~13.html.

2. NAPO, 2009 Get Organized Month Survey, June 30, 2009, www.napo.net.

3. Dana Knight, "*USA Today*, Consequences of Messy Desks," *The Indianapolis Star*, January 22, 2006.

4. The Surprising Health & Psychological Benefits of a Clean, Uncluttered Desk, Study by Open Ergonomics on behalf of NEC Mitsubishi, November 2, 2005.

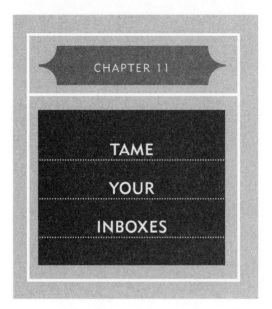

CHAPTER 11

TAME

YOUR

INBOXES

"I have a theory about the human mind. A brain is a lot like a computer. It

will only take so many facts, and then it will go on overload and blow up."

—ERMA BOMBECK

Flash back a decade or two. Communicating in the 1990s was a much simpler proposition. You had one email address, an answering machine, and a regular, good old-fashioned mailbox. It was okay to take a day or two to respond to an email, only doctors got paged, text messages were nonexistent, blackberries were something you ate, and twittering was something little birds did. Clearly a lot has changed!

Today, we're all grappling with inbox overload. The typical person we spoke with had no fewer than six inboxes to check: two email accounts, at least one snail mail box, two or three voice mail boxes, and at least one, but typically two, social networking accounts. Look around you and it's not uncommon to see someone checking their mobile device to read email, respond to a text message, take a call, or all three—all while trying to do something else, like watch a child's soccer game. There are just so many ways to communicate these days that staying on top of incoming messages has become a constant stress. If you fall behind, which can happen quickly when emails accumulate at the rate of one hundred or more a day, digging out from under them is no less arduous than digging out from under a mountain of physical clutter. A December 2007 *New York Times* blog post described email as "a $650 Billion Drag on the Economy,"[1] and the *New York Times* reported in April 2008 that "email has become the bane of some people's professional lives due to information overload."[2] Unfortunately, the article concludes that until there is some magic software invented to help us prepare replies, the problem of inbox overload isn't going to go away. If anything, it's just going to get worse—because the number of ways in which we communicate is growing, not shrinking.

A UNIVERSAL PROBLEM

Julie Otis Waltzer, a corporate event planner living in San Francisco, suffers from a bad case of inbox overload that started spiraling out of control last summer when she launched her own special events company just two months after marrying her longtime boyfriend, Ben.

"Between my expanding client list and my new last name, I am on email overload. I check four email addresses constantly throughout the day: my work email, my freelance email, and my personal emails—one with my maiden name and one with my married name. My phone is an even bigger nightmare—inevitably, when I finally get a moment to clear the messages off my voice mail, another call comes in while I'm stuck listening to eighteen other messages. How am I ever going to keep in contact without inbox management becoming a full-time job?"

Julie's case of "inbox overload" isn't unusual. We simply have too many inboxes and too little time. Darcy Ahl, busy working mother to three, says that managing all of it makes her crazy at times. "Every now and then I get frustrated and just hold down the delete button. I think I've got about 1,400 emails in my various inboxes at any given moment. I try to print out important stuff and put it into the appropriate files, but the sheer volume is overwhelming. I've got filters set up, so there's not even much spam in there.

It's all real stuff. I wish there was a better way to stay on top of it, but I sure haven't found it yet. I'm ready to pull the plug altogether."

Helene Kornsgold, a rabbi and counselor living in Los Angeles, struggles to keep up with the ever-changing modes of communication. "It's just hard for me to organize something I can't physically touch. I'm completely behind the curve when it comes to staying on top of my inbox. As soon as I have one thing under control, another mode of communication pops up and it starts all over. Last month I missed a friend's son's baby-naming because she'd posted it on Facebook. I know I sound like an old woman, but when did Facebook take the place of email? It must have been right after email took the place of actual invitations! I'm never going to get on top of this."

Dealing with the inundation of communication is stressful, and that stress spills over into all areas of life. A study by Reuters on the impact of information overload found that 42 percent of people claimed it was making them physically ill and 60 percent said that the data onslaught makes them "frequently too tired for leisure activities" and much more likely to "cancel social activities," too.[3] That's simply no way to live. Of course, cutting off contact with the outside world isn't really a viable option for any of us.

You've got to learn to manage your inbox, to simplify, and to regain control of the communication that comes your way. Now that's a tall order. Fortunately, a few of your peers have come up with some ingenious solutions for keeping communication under control. We'll show you how they did it, and how you can do it, too.

STRENGTHENING YOUR IM (INBOX MANAGEMENT) MUSCLES

When your inbox is out of shape it slows you down, wasting precious time and stressing you out. But there is hope. With a little elbow grease, your inboxes can go from cluttered to clean, once again becoming tools that help you stay informed and on top of your game. The goal is to regain control of the information flowing your way each day. Taking three simple steps will whip your inbox into shape:

1. Set clear parameters.
2. Pare down unnecessary volume.
3. Establish simple systems.

SET CLEAR PARAMETERS

When it comes to managing your inbox, less is definitely more. You can't possibly keep up with hundreds and thousands of messages coming at you from every possible device without (a) turning your focus away from what you really want to be concentrating on, (b) going gray, and (c) feeling overwhelmed. The first step to regaining some semblance of control is to set parameters—for yourself and for others. That means cutting down on the number of modes you use to communicate. Here's how some smart folks have done just that to great effect.

Sara Gives Up on Snail Mail

According to Forest Ethics, there are one hundred billion pieces of junk mail sent to Americans each year—that's an average of eight hundred pieces per person. We waste lots of time sorting through it all to get to the one or two pieces of real mail. Sara Schofield, a busy mom to two and part-time nurse, got tired of dealing with the mail pile each day and decided to eliminate it altogether. "I just got tired of having to sit down and sift through the myriad catalogs, credit card offers, and other junk every night after the kids went to bed. If I skipped a day, it would pile up on my counter and I'd stress about losing a bill or something important. So I decided to stop dealing with it. I went online and signed up to get e-statements for all of my accounts. Now I get all of my bills via email. I also let all of my friends know not to send me invitations or thank you notes in the mail—but to save the stamp and send me an email instead. I moved my mailbox to a side of the house that was two steps from the garbage cans. Now I open the mailbox, take everything that's inside, and toss it immediately. I don't look at one scrap of it and I haven't missed anything important yet."

Hollie Trims Her Social Networking Roster

When Hollie Sehrt graduated from Parsons School of Design and joined Buttoned Up, she was facing so many firsts in her life—first job, first apartment, first car, and first Internet addiction: Facebook. "I completely acknowledge that social networking is a huge time suck for me, but it's important for me to stay connected to my friends, and so I was hooked. Still, I know I just don't have the bandwidth to deal with all of it—Facebook, MySpace, LinkedIn, and Twitter—so I scaled back in two ways. First, I canceled all the other social networking sights except Facebook and Twitter. Second, I started limiting myself to checking-in just two times a day, and no more. That way I can update my status and keep a presence without shirking all of my other responsibilities."

Julie Designates Texts for Family Only

Julie Papadopoulos, entrepreneur and new mom, lives in fast-paced New York City. Her job as an event planner and organizer requires her to be at the beck and call of her clients. As text messaging gained in popularity, her clients had a tendency to overwhelm her with them. "I knew it was getting out of hand when I twisted my ankle for the third time in about as many weeks because I was trying to text *and* run errands at the same time. I decided enough was enough—texting was clearly hazardous to my health! I instituted a new rule with all of my clients: texting was off limits. I would respond to texts from my family only. If they needed to reach me quickly, they could call my cell phone instead. The amazing thing is that it's been a faster and far better way to communicate. My clients and I waste far less time. You think a text is going to be faster, but the moment you have to get additional information or clarity on something, which is nearly always the case, the back and forth can get out of control and really suck up a lot of time."

The ironic thing about paring down your accepted channels is that it requires a little additional communication on your part. You have to let the people you actually *want* to communicate with know which channels to reach you by and which to avoid. The good news is that people typically respond very positively because they are often dealing with the same overload and looking for ways to get their inboxes under control as well.

REDUCE UNNECESSARY VOLUME

Once you've set clear parameters around the devices you will use to stay in touch with others, it's time to focus on getting the sheer volume of communiqués under control. Thus, step two involves letting others (including listservs and databases) know when they are crossing the line and sending too many unnecessary messages. Here are a few ways others are doing just that.

Kim Reduces Reply-to-All Offenders
Kim Davis, a financial advisor living in Manhattan, has found an effective way to pare down the volume of unnecessary email that costs her valuable time and some of her sanity as well. "My worst inbox stuffers are all those people who hit 'reply-all' on a message that should only go to one recipient. I find that a huge number of emails in my inbox really don't really concern me. Before long, I have a million back-and-forth emails discussing who-knows-what that are taking up space in my inbox. It makes me want to scream, 'Don't send me an email that doesn't concern me!' So I'm trying an experiment. Whenever I send an email to a group of people, I always include at the bottom: 'Please keep our inboxes uncluttered. Only hit reply-all if you need everyone to read your response.' It hasn't completely curbed the reply-all emails I receive, but it has helped. I've also noticed that a few friends and colleagues are starting to put the same message in their emails as well. Hopefully it will become an unwritten rule of email conduct in the future."

A Pretty Neat Tip

RSS FEEDS

Emails from your favorite news sources and blogs are a great way to stay in the loop—but those same emails can clog your inbox in short order. RSS feeds, like Google Reader, offer a free, easy-to-use alternative. RSS stands for "really simple syndication" and all it does is aggregate feeds from websites and blogs you want to track. Typically "new" news and posts are displayed on one summary page, so you can see what's going on with one quick glance. They also make it easy to share interesting content with other people. For more information about Google Reader, visit www.googlereader.blogspot.com.

Megan Unsubscribes Her Way to Inbox Organization
As soon as Megan Chin, a dentist living in San Francisco, purchased her Blackberry, she realized that the volume of emails she received each day was out of control. "Getting my Blackberry was a blessing and a curse. I had no idea how many listservs and newsletters and advertisements I got each day. My phone was buzzing nonstop all the time, and it drove me crazy at first. I seriously considered going back to my old email-free phone. But then I decided that I needed to cut the junk, and within a few weeks, I'd unsubscribed to 90 percent of the lists I was on because I was just sick of

being notified about this and that. My rule of thumb is that if I haven't worn something in six months it gets donated, and if I haven't opened an email from a certain sender in three months, then it's time to unsubscribe. It takes two seconds to do it in the moment. Now when I get an email it's usually worth reading."

Rosemary Avoids Spam with a "Shopping-Only" Email

Rosemary Biagioni, a busy working mom with two grown boys, focuses on the important stuff in her email by sending the unimportant stuff elsewhere. "I've got two primary email addresses that I check constantly—work and personal—but I also created an extra one that's just for buying stuff online. I don't want my main inboxes to be bombarded with advertisements and newsletters from every place I've ever shopped, so I only use that extra address for online purchases. It's great because I can easily sign into that account and find coupons and old orders when I want (which isn't all that often), without clogging my inbox."

If your first instinct is to hit delete when you see something hit your inbox, know that taking two seconds to respond or unsubscribe now will save you time, sanity, and inbox space down the line.

ESTABLISH SIMPLE SYSTEMS

Once you've pared down, it's time to put some simple systems in place to maintain some semblance of control over the long haul. The great news is that there are a variety of simple, low-tech things you can do to keep inboxes organized. Another plus: Technology makes it pretty easy to filter out the noise so you can zero in on what is really important.

Rachel Institutes a YUNK Folder for Email Stragglers

Rachel Wiser's position as a university administrator means that an overwhelming number of emails come her way every day, and the majority of them must be addressed immediately. Still, a small percentage of emails can't be dealt with right away, and those are the ones that end up clogging her inbox and distracting her from the important ones. "Clearly, cutting down the thousands of emails in my inbox is vital, so I set up efolders—nothing revolutionary about that—and I file things away as soon as I've completed them. What's still in my inbox works as my to-do list. Then I noticed that what I couldn't tend to immediately started clogging up my inbox. I kept thinking, 'What if I need this later?' and that kept me from deleting any

Meet: Roxanne Lott

Family: Married

Occupation: Cofounder of Imerex, a marketing agency

Q: How many inboxes do you currently manage?

A: I've got eight inboxes all together—plus Facebook, Twitter, and LinkedIn. I have a regular snail mailbox at home. I have three voice mails that I check, three different email accounts, and then the social networking stuff.

Q: What are the worst inbox offenders?

A: Well, because I'm in a service industry—I'd have to say clients! Not only do I get regular emails, but I am actually on the customer email list for a bunch of my clients so we can see what their customers are seeing. I have to go through and eyeball those as well. Then there's this whole social media thing. I really enjoy Facebook— it's a great way to keep up with people I don't see very often. But I get to do it on my terms. Twitter, well, it just astounds me with the noise it produces. That's probably my single biggest offender. Yet, I feel like I have to do it because of the line of work I'm in.

Q: How do you stay on top of your inbox?

A: The key to managing it all for me is filing everything as it comes in. I use a program called SimplyFile that works with my Microsoft Outlook program. It learns which folders all of my emails go into, and with one click I can send them there. It's great. I am the kind of person that needs to 'touch' every email before filing it away, but all I have to do is click the File Message button in the program and the email automatically goes into the appropriate file. I also have auto filters set up so that the newsletters and customer marketing emails I have to monitor go directly into folders without my having to look at them first. All in, I probably have forty-five to fifty folders in my Outlook. My inbox is clean and uncluttered, which I love.

Q: With so many inboxes to check, what gives?

A: Voice mail. I hate checking it, and people that call my cell know not to leave me a message because my phone will tell me that you called. Texting helps too. It's much faster and better. I don't get that much voice mail as a result, and that's fine with me.

A Pretty Neat Tip

HOW TO CUT THE VIRTUAL JUNK

Virtual junk mail may not take up space in your mailbox or recycle bin, but it can clog up your inbox and keep you from getting to the important stuff. When spam, ads, and newsletters start to take over, it's time to cut the junk.

1. Unsubscribe. Most advertisements and newsletters come with an unsubscribe button at the bottom of the email. Clicking that link should remove your email address within ten days. If messages continue to come, this is a violation of the CAN-SPAM Act, and you can file a complaint at www.ftc.gov/spam/.

2. Set up spam filters. According to spamlaws.com, more than 80 percent of all email is spam. Setting up filters is a great way to curb spam. If your work email is being spammed, let your technology staff know so they can update the filters for your office.

3. Get a second email address. Signing up for an additional email address is a good way to keep your personal email private. You can give out the second email address, and let the spam find its way there instead.

4. Read the privacy policy. If the company's fine print acknowledges that they share or sell your email, then don't give it your address. If there's an option to keep your information private, do that; but if not, look elsewhere or suffer the spam-filled consequences.

email that I might need eventually. So I created a YUNK (you never know) folder to save stuff for a rainy day. Now I put all my you-never-know emails in the YUNK folder, and I can focus on the important stuff that remains in my inbox."

Leslie Takes Advantage of Gmail Functionality
Leslie Carothers, owner of the Kaleidoscope Partnership, a social media community management company for the home furnishings industry, and writer of FurnitureToday.com's Retail Ideas blog, keeps her eye on the ball by using some simple but effective Gmail functionality-filters and labels. "I put filters on all my incoming mail so instead of hitting my inbox, the email goes straight to the relevant folder. Not seeing so many scattered subject

lines in my inbox, just nicely organized messages in their relevant folders, makes me feel calmer. I can choose when to 'deep dive' into that folder so I can focus completely—minimizing the chances I'll get distracted by another incoming email. If an incoming email isn't part of a filter category I've set up, then I use Gmail's labels. Gmail allows you to attach labels of your own choosing to every email and then color-code them. With color-coding, I can know at a glance what I want to zero in on and what can wait until later. Using filters and colored labels has made it *very* easy to work in a calmer, more focused, and efficient manner with a corresponding dramatic improvement on my productivity levels!"

Amy Sticks to a Regular Check-In Routine

Amy Lerner, a busy wife, mother, and business owner, spends her days—and many late nights—working in front of her computer. She estimates that, on an average day, three hundred or so emails flood her inbox. To stay on top of it, she set up a check-in routine. "I can't leave my email open all day or I'd do nothing but read emails. Instead, first thing in the morning, I go through my inbox and flag the emails that have to get taken care of that day. After that, I have my email program download new emails just a few times a day, rather than every five minutes. My current schedule is to download emails at noon, 2:30 PM, and 5 PM. I have set a permanent thirty-minute appointment with myself at each of the download time windows so that I can spend some uninterrupted time to go through and respond and sort through the new emails. Because I'm not trying to multitask; I have time to read every email immediately and flag it as a task to complete today, move it to an appropriate folder to deal with later, or delete it. It's made me substantially more efficient."

It's safe to assume that 20 percent of the information that makes it into your inbox is critical and the remaining 80 percent is not. Put systems in place that make it easy to identify the truly important incoming materials, phone calls, emails, and

A Pretty Neat Tip

SIMPLE SOCIAL NETWORKING

Social networking sites keep us connected socially and professionally. But they also can be a huge time suck. These tips will help you reap the benefits of networking without giving up all your time.

1. Limit yourself to signing in once or twice a day.

2. Forward important notifications to your personal email.

3. Don't post anything you wouldn't want your boss to see.

4. Don't use the default alert settings—turn off the ones that don't interest you.

5. Feel free to "unfriend."

other data. You can use technological filters to identify significant data, set up basic folders, have others sift through the detritus for you, or evaluate it on the fly.

CHAPTER WRAP-UP

You can connect with anyone you want in virtually any way you choose, twenty-four hours a day, seven days a week. Unfortunately, inboxes are a bit like major highways—the more lanes they build, the more traffic grows; the more inboxes you have, the more information you receive. You can take control in three simple steps.

- *Set Clear Parameters:* The first step to regaining some semblance of control is to set parameters—for yourself and for others. That means cutting down on the number of modes you use to communicate. That might mean ditching your home phone, selecting one dominant technological format for receiving information, or banning instant messaging.

- *Reduce Unnecessary Volume:* You can't focus on the important stuff when you're inundated with messages you don't really need or want. Get the sheer volume of communiqués under control by letting others (including listservs and databases) know when they are crossing the line and sending too many unnecessary messages.

- *Establish Simple Systems:* Set up a simple, easy-to-manage system that keeps your inbox organized. Creating basic file folders, using filters, and following a regular clean-out routine will ensure that your system works for you.

---

1. Steve Lohr. "Is Information Overload a $650 Billion Drag on the Economy?" *New York Times,* December 12, 2007.

2. Randall Stross. "Struggling to Evade the E-Mail Tsunami," *New York Times,* April 20, 2008.

3. P. Waddington, "Dying for Information? A report on the effects of information overload in the UK and worldwide," 1997, www.cni.org/regconfs/1997/ukoln-content/rep~13.html.

CHAPTER 12

MASTER

HOME-COOKED

MEALS (REALLY!)

"The most remarkable thing about my mother is that for 30 years she served

the family nothing but leftovers. The original meal has never been found."

—CALVIN TRILLIN

There's getting a meal on the table and there's getting a *real* meal on the table. And boy, at the end of a long day, trying to get a relatively healthy *real* meal on the table can be one of the most challenging things to do. Skipping it isn't really an option, because to some degree or another we all need to get a little nightly nourishment. So at around 4:30 or 5:00 PM on any given weekday, the dance begins. First there's the question of *what*, which when you're tired and not feeling terribly creative, or if you have picky eaters at home, or if your pantry is empty, can be harder to figure out than it seems. Then there's the actual preparation. The last thing most people want to do is walk in the door and spend the next hour and a half slaving over a hot stove. Thirty minutes is about all we want to spare on the cooking front, thank you very much. So where does that leave us? A few people seem to have a knack for whipping up something yummy and healthy to eat. But as far as we can see, that's not the norm.

WHAT'S FOR DINNER?

Sarah Welch, co-author and cofounder of Buttoned Up, mother to two boys, and champion of the imperfectly organized, loves food. But when it comes to getting herself organized to get a relatively healthy weeknight dinner on the table, it's another story.

"I keep hoping that I'll get a grip on the whole preparing-a-healthy-weeknight-dinner thing while my kids are still young. So far, I'm more of an appreciator of good food than a creator of it. I typically have a bowl of cereal or oatmeal with my son at 7:00 AM and then I sort of forget about food during the day when I'm working. I might have a yogurt, apple, and Diet Coke somewhere around 1:30 PM. If I'm starving, I'll raid the vending machine and have a Twix or Hershey's chocolate bar with almonds. Mmmm. Anyhoo . . . next thing I know it's 5:30 PM—time to race home— and on the drive home, I have the oh-my-God-what-are-we-going-to-eat-tonight thought, and then I walk in the door, realize how hungry I am, and head straight for the easiest thing to prepare so that dinner can be on the table minutes later. Often that means grabbing the rotisserie chicken from the fridge and reheating it with some quick-cook rice. Pasta's always a good standby, too. If our son Will hasn't eaten yet, I'll make sure we get a veggie in the meal. If not, I'll let it slide—maybe three times out of five I'll get one in there. I'm not above frozen pizzas or frozen dinner entrées either (I can see my parents, who worked so hard to instill healthy eating habits in us, recoiling in horror as they read this).

"The fact of the matter is, I'm a suburban-dwelling, working mother to two. I just don't have a lot of time or energy to spare. At least that's what I tell myself. Each and every week, sometimes on Sunday, sometimes on Monday, I have a fleeting fantasy that *this is the week* I'll figure it all out and whip up five or six deliciously healthy dinners without breaking a sweat. But by Friday I'm right back where I started. In the deep recesses of my mind, I know I'm just rationalizing . . . but I just can't seem to get far enough ahead of it to be able to make it work."

After a long day in the trenches, most of us are like Sarah: too tired, too overwhelmed, and too full of doubt in our own capabilities to do anything more than just muddle through the evening meal (can we say, "Bowl of cereal for dinner, anyone?"). Like Sarah, are we just rationalizing our behavior? Let's take a look at what we heard were the biggest impediments to getting a good meal on the table.

I DON'T HAVE ENOUGH TIME OR ENERGY

Lack of time is a very real issue. The census bureau reports that for the first time in history, both parents work in the majority of married families with children. Regardless of marital status, as of the last census, 73 percent of the 31.3 million mothers ages fifteen to forty-four whose children were older than a year worked.[1] Rather than staying at home, preparing meals, and waiting for the kids to come home from school, the majority of moms are out there commuting, working, and sometimes logging extra hours at night. Stay-at-home moms are working harder too. There are many more extracurricular activities today than there were even ten years ago, which is exhausting in its own right. Stress is also an issue. Males and females all agree we're more stressed at work today than we were a generation ago.[2] No wonder we feel too tired and overwhelmed to cook!

Marci Miller sums up the dilemma perfectly: "I have four kids, ages five to thirteen, and my afternoons are spent running them around from place to place. By the time it gets to dinner time I just want to get something, really *anything*, on the table so we can finish homework and get to bed. I know I should be more concerned about homemade meals and planning out things, but I just don't have the energy."

I HAVE PICKY EATERS

Picky eaters also make dinner prep more stressful. If you have to go out of your way to accommodate limited palates, it can be the thing that puts you over the edge and causes you to give up on serving a good meal altogether. Angela Harris struggles with a finicky eater. "I have two boys, ages nine and eleven, and one of them in particular is very picky. He likes bean dip, chicken nuggets, and a few fruits and vegetables. I have given up trying to get him to eat different things."

She's so not alone. Bea Welch's youngest son eats only buttered pasta . . . and nothing, I mean *nothing*, green. Kathleen Ferguson's third son eats chicken quesadillas and occasionally chicken nuggets, hold the veggies and the fruit. Beth Eyon's oldest daughter only ate chicken nuggets, grapes, and pita-bread pizzas until a few months ago, when she expanded her palate to include cantaloupe. On and on it goes.

It's not just kids who are picky, either. Anne Marie Furie has a picky husband, which makes her dinner prep a particular challenge. "First off, he's allergic to poultry, which happened midmarriage, so 80 percent of my menu repertoire went out the window right there. He doesn't like lamb. He doesn't like pork, and he doesn't really care for fish. That leaves me with beef and vegetables, and he doesn't really love vegetables. And he's got heart problems, so there's only so much beef the man can have! He'll eat asparagus, which is only really in season in the spring—otherwise I have to resort to canned or frozen. I've found that I get him to eat veggies if I mask them in a taco salad or something like that. All this dancing around food limitations is a challenge. I used to be a really good cook, but I'm not anymore. I've fallen out of habit."

Kate Loreto's husband doesn't do salads. "The first time I made him a big, beautiful salad, he looked at me sweetly and asked where the real dinner was. He said, 'Baby, I am not a goat. I do not eat this stuff!' It was pretty funny . . . but it also means I don't eat salads too often for dinner anymore."

Experts call our tendency to cook around picky palates the "pampered palate syndrome." Some evenings, it means whoever is doing the cooking will prepare at least two, and often three or four, different meals. Even then, getting family members to eat can be a battle. No wonder we don't want to face the dinner hour.

I DON'T KNOW HOW TO COOK

A lot of people we spoke with along the way just plum never learned to cook. Take Susan Belle for example. "I am not a natural cook . . . I just never learned when I was younger. I was too busy with school, sports, and my piano playing. Now I have to look up how to cook rice, for heaven's sakes— I'd be toast without that boxed stuff with the directions on the side! I'm way too intimidated to cook from scratch, and vegetables don't really come with directions, so I go for the frozen stuff."

Maybe Susan's an extreme example. The fact of the matter is a lot of people lack confidence in their ability to cook anything. Perhaps that is due to the fact that this is the first generation of adults whose mothers worked and lacked the time or energy to teach their kids how to cook. Perhaps it has to do with the fact that home economics was phased out in our schools.

A Pretty Neat Tip

BE QUICKER IN THE KITCHEN

Karen Kelly, a writer and editor with a two-and-a-half-year-old son, keeps her kitchen utensils streamlined so she doesn't waste time hunting for the things she uses most often.

"We always have a salad as a side dish for dinner—every night. I keep my salad bowl in a cabinet on the lower shelf, right above the prep counter. I keep it right at eye level, which I'm sure a professional decorator would tell me is exactly the wrong spot for it. But it's always within arm's reach.

"I also keep my key salad utensils inside the bowl—including my whisk and two kinds of graters. I used to have to dig through my utensil drawer for them, which is a few steps away, and every time I pulled out the whisk, at least three other utensils would fly out at the same time, so I'd have to pick them up and put them away.

"Now all I have to do is pull the salad bowl down off the shelf and I'm ready to go. The only other thing I need is the paring knife, which is in the knife holder on the same counter I prepare the salad—so no extra reaching. I know that just by organizing these few items, I save at least five minutes a night. That adds up to a lot over time!"

Perhaps it has to do with a lack of desire. Whatever the reason, if you think you don't know how to cook, you're not going to go out of your way to cook anything you deem difficult at mealtime.

THE SIREN CALL OF PROCESSED FOODS

To get by, we increasingly rely on processed, packaged, and semiprepared food, as well as takeout, to help us get something on the table quickly and relatively easily. We've seen articles online that claim that for every dollar Americans spend on food, 90 cents is spent on processed foods. We don't know about that, but in a rigorous study conducted at UCLA's Center on Everyday Lives of Families, researchers videotaped thirty-two families, including their dinner routines, for a three-year period, from 2002 through 2005. Although 70 percent of the dinners were home-cooked, most included moderate amounts of packaged food. Ironically, the same study found that the use of processed, commercial foods did not meaningfully reduce the amount of time spent cooking. Using processed shortcuts saved an average of ten to twelve minutes of hands-on time but did not reduce the total fifty-two minutes of average preparation time. The illusion is that because it does reduce the amount of prep work, such as peeling, chopping, and mixing, it's faster.[3] Sadly, it's just unhealthier.

Fortunately, there are plenty of people who have figured out ways to make healthy weeknight meals at home, quickly. Examining their tricks made us realize it doesn't take any more effort, really, to prepare a healthy meal than it does to prepare a less healthy one.

HOW TO HIT THE TRIFECTA: HEALTHY, GOOD, AND EASY

What is the secret of healthy cooking—especially on weeknights? Well, how do you get to Carnegie Hall? Practice, practice, practice. When it comes to getting this weeknight meal thing down, practice really does make the entire thing much, much easier. That's the first step. The second, third, and fourth steps: streamline, streamline, streamline. And finally: Have a backup plan.

PRACTICE, PRACTICE, PRACTICE

The first few times you cook anything, whether it's a simple Caesar salad or vegetable lasagna, it's going to take some time. You'll have to look up the recipe, carefully read the ingredients list to make sure you have what you need, and then closely follow the preparation instructions. You'll probably check the recipe multiple times during the cooking process, too, which will also slow you down. If you get something wrong, you might even have to start over. But the more you prepare something, the easier (and faster) it becomes to make. The people who are naturally good at preparing healthy meals quickly didn't get there overnight. They practiced making the good dishes often enough that it became second nature.

Teresita Reyes, a baby nurse, has been cooking the same fifteen to twenty recipes for the past thirty years. "I probably have more or less around fifteen recipes in my head—some are 'mix and match' in the sense that I know this dish can go with that one and that one, so the fifteen recipes add up to more than fifteen different menus, if that makes sense. Sort of like how you have a black pair of pants that will go with a few different things, so you have more than just one outfit. I have been making these dishes for about twenty-five to thirty years now. Obviously, when I first started, it used to take me a lot longer to prepare. Now I can do them automatically, which means my mind is free to think about and do other things. Shopping is easier too. I always know what to get because I know what I am going to cook."

Janet Smith, program director for a Transcendental Meditation center, wife, and stepmother to three, is devoted to serving fresh food, freshly prepared. She never has leftovers or uses packed, canned, or frozen foods. Sound impossible? Not with a little practice. "I work full time, and often on evenings and weekends too, so I don't have a lot of spare time to spend cooking elaborate dinners. My secret is that I cook the same staples over and over again. That's number one! My staples are grains and beans. For somebody else, it might be chicken and rice. Once I pick a grain/bean combination from my roster (which is easy since I prepare them all the time), all I really have to decide what to cook is the vegetable. The vegetable is what freshens up the meal and keeps the menu feeling different enough over time. I look for what's in season, what's in the fridge, what's in the garden. There are really only three ways to prepare most veggies: steam, sauté, or boil. Once you have those basic cooking techniques down, it gets easier and easier. In addition, I really strive to keep the overall meal simple. Each dish or course you add increases its complexity. So I stick to more basic, simple foods. I don't do the more elaborate things unless I have the time."

Susan Bachtelle also succeeds at eating healthily by keeping it simple and having a routine. "We always know what we're going to eat for dinner—a big, huge salad. My fiancée makes it during the late afternoon at some point and we dress it at dinner and have it with a glass of wine."

Of course, you have to start somewhere. Marie Dennis, working mom to six, is a brilliant improviser in the kitchen now, but that wasn't always the case. "I'm definitely an improviser now. But when my children were really little, I had a menu that I wrote for a month. I had to have one for every day of the year, partly because we lived on a farm that was nowhere near a grocery store, but also because I worked and found it impossible to come home and then have 'Yikes, what are we going to eat?' I made a menu that made the best use of what we had in the house and/or what was growing at the time. In the end, I had one master food calendar for an entire year. I didn't set out to do it; I did it a month at a time, but at the end of twelve months, I realized I had one for a year. It was great when the kids were little—I just followed it without having to think too hard. As they got older, the plan also was great because it meant they could start dinner before I got home, and that was obviously very handy. Today, I can make anything on that yearly menu pretty much from memory, on autopilot."

Meet: Tamra Davis

Family: Married with two children

Occupation: Film and TV director (*Billy Madison, Grey's Anatomy*), founder/creator of TheTamraDavisCookingShow.com, and author of *Make Me Something Good to Eat.*

Q: When it comes to cooking healthy dinners, are you a planner or an improviser?

A: Cooking and directing are very similar. Putting on a Thanksgiving dinner, or any dinner for that matter, is exactly like directing a movie. You do have to have a plan for the meal, even if it's a loose one. But then, when you're actually cooking, you have to let go and just enjoy it. That is what translates to a good dish. So I'd say, yes, I have a general game plan, but then I try to have fun while I'm going for it in the moment.

Q: Do you make a menu plan for the week?

A: When my kids were younger, I definitely had a menu planned out for the week. As a working mom, I think it's harder if you don't have that plan. Not only are you tired and probably not at your most creative when you walk in the door after a long day, but you also have to be prepared for nights when someone else, like a sitter, is cooking for your kids. Having a menu planned out just makes it that much easier to eat healthily—it gives you more control over what everyone is eating. Now that my kids are a little older, both my sitter and I know the routine and the recipes, so I don't need as tight a menu plan as before, but I still do some planning, mostly on the weekend. I usually try to cook a few things on Saturday and Sunday that the kids can have during the week—planning leftovers is always good.

Q: As someone who has figured out how to cook healthy dinners (and get your kids to eat them), what kinds of things would you recommend to someone who is still trying to figure it out?

A: First, and probably most important, keep it simple and go slowly. Start to build your repertoire with one or two items you feel comfortable cooking, like pasta. Learn how to make a simple, healthy pasta dish. Just one. Then make it again next week, and the week after that, and the week after that, too. Before you know it, making that dish will be second nature; you'll know the required ingredients and won't have to consult a cookbook for directions. Once you're there, learn to make another one, and another one.

If you're looking for ways to cut down your prep time, take some knife lessons at a local culinary school. You only have to take one class, one time. But I promise, just knowing how to cut can take your prep time from an hour down to twenty minutes. It's so basic and will make a world of difference.

If you're struggling to synchronize your cooking so that everything is simultaneously ready and warm, cook your protein last. In general, protein either cooks up really fast or really slow, and usually the former. It's pretty easy to keep grain warm, so do that ahead of time. Having one less thing on at the same time will give you room to focus your attention on the protein, and since that's the center of the meal, it's what you want to get right.

As far as vegetables are concerned, I have two tricks. First, I plan family meals for nights when I know the farmer's market will be open. That way I can stop on my way to/from something and get some fresh items. Second, I make soups a lot. I have a recipe for making a basic veggie soup that works with *any* kind of veggie you've got in your fridge. So if I've got celery or carrots or any other vegetable that is looking a little long in the tooth, I throw it in the pot and voilà, I've got a healthy dinner and didn't waste anything.

Q: What about getting your kids to eat what you make? What's the trick?

A: Well, it's just got to be about fun. I find that letting kids *name* a dish gets them into it. For example, if I'm making a pesto pasta dish, I'll tell them, "Hey guys, I'm making a green pasta—let's come up with a name for it." They'll come up with things like "Shrek Pasta" or "Hulk Pasta" or "Squidworld Pasta." That goes down a lot easier. Another time, I really wanted them to eat a strawberry fruit smoothie I made for them. I knew they wouldn't eat anything pink if left to their own devices, but once they named it "The Weirdo Milkshake"—it was gone! Other things you can do: Make a drawing or write their name on the plate with ketchup. Shape the grain with their initials. Use something like peas to make a face on the protein or grain. Anything that makes food fun, works.

Another thing kids like is routine. We make specific dishes on certain days. Saturday we always make pancakes for breakfast. Sunday, we always have scrambled eggs and bagels. On Wednesday mornings, we have French toast. Fridays are pizza days.

It's amazing how a little bit of practice can make something that was once complicated and time-consuming easier. Start small, make up one or two healthy menus, and master the dishes in each. Then gradually add new ones to your repertoire. The next thing you know, you'll be a pro.

STREAMLINE, STREAMLINE, STREAMLINE

To make their workout harder, Olympic-caliber swimmers typically practice wearing three or four swimsuits to create extra drag. Then when it counts, they streamline; instead of three or four old suits, they'll put on one super-skintight suit and maybe even shave their entire body, so that nothing extraneous slows them down. Time matters, down to a hundredth of a second. Time matters for busy cooks too!

The second trick of those who magically throw together healthy meals is that they look to reduce drag anywhere they can. They streamline their what's-for-dinner process by making a plan for the week, preferably with help from others. They streamline their shopping with lists and, where available, computer ordering. They streamline their prep by having essential tools within arm's reach.

Lacey Pappas works full time and manages to cook healthy meals at home at least four nights a week. "The best tip to make things easier during the week is to plan ahead. On Saturday I get out the recipe books and plan at least four meals. I make a list and shop on the weekend so I don't have to worry about it during the week when I am crazed. Then I know all the stuff is at home, and it motivates me to go home and actually cook!"

Author Michelle Garrison Hough, mom to two toddlers, streamlines with the help of her husband, Jamie. "I'm in charge of the meals during the week, or sometimes we will make things together on the weekends and then heat them up on weekdays. That's pretty much how it goes. Jamie also has a funny quirk that helps keep me on track: He likes to make lists for me. Some Saturdays he will make me a list with meals for each night, and then he will make a grocery store list that allows me to practically run through the store at top speed. He organizes the shopping list by sections of the store. The bottom right hand corner of the list has the meals for the week listed, so that when I bring the list home from the store I tear off the bottom corner and attach it to the fridge with a magnet."

Kerry Lyons, mom to five under five and full-time marketing executive for an Internet startup, also relies on a plan for the week to reduce the drag. "Pre-triplets, as long as I knew I had ingredients, I was fine to improvise. Now I really have to plan everything out, which seems like it would take more time, but it saves me loads in the long run. It doesn't really take me that long to plan for the week because I do a lot of repeats. Having a plan means I can cut corners by doing all the pre-prep on Sunday afternoons—because when I walk in the door at 5:00 PM on a weeknight, everybody has to be fed within thirty minutes of my arrival. Plus, as long as I plan it, my husband, Des, will cook it. But if I don't plan it, he's lost. Having a plan also lets me see ahead to opportunities where I can cook two dinners at once, like chicken breasts—we can do them on the grill and make enough for two dinners."

Gina Bernstein, working mom to three, also streamlines with a plan. "I do all the planning, usually when I'm at the grocery store, which is a really bad time to do it! But one of the things I did was to take all of my favorite recipes, copy them, and put them in a small spiral notebook. It's small enough to keep in my car's glove compartment, so I always have it available to me at the grocery store and I always know what ingredients are needed. I also have a general rule of thumb for dish rotation: My rule is one meat, one chicken, one fish, one pasta every week. Just having that general rule makes my dinner routine a lot easier."

Janet Smith streamlines her shopping, something she hates to do. "I try to be very organized when it comes to shopping—it's fine that I have to do the cooking, but I don't want to go shopping too! So I buy staples, like my whole grains, legumes/beans, raisins, spices, baking supplies, and cleaning products in bulk (three to six months at a time). I buy them in twenty-five-pound bags and store them in lidded bins. These items don't spoil so I always have them on hand for last-minute meals. I also found a store that lets me put my order in online, via computer. I keep a grocery list just for my staples right on their site, which means I never forget anything. The first time setting it up takes some time, but once you're set up, then it's really quick. I point, click, and then drive to the store to pick it up. It's a huge time-saver for me."

There are many ways to streamline your dinner routine without having to compromise on the quality of food you're eating. Keep your eyes peeled for them and implement them wherever you can.

PLAN FOR "OFF" NIGHTS

Let's face it, there are going to be days that just suck the wind out of you. On those days, there is just no way you're going to want to cook. Have a "free" night scheduled into the week, just in case. Know what your healthy backup plan is—whether it's reheating something frozen you made earlier, eating leftovers, or ordering a pizza, so you're not heading out for super-fatty fast food at the eleventh hour.

CHAPTER WRAP-UP

Many people have a secret fantasy of being able to pull off home-cooked meals five nights a week. But somehow, putting together a meal can be the most challenging thing to do after a long day in the trenches. Is there any

A Pretty Neat Tip

SIMPLE SHORTCUTS TO HEALTHIER EATING

•Prep Healthy Snacks in Advance: On Sunday night after all the little ones are in bed asleep, grab a few carrots, a cucumber, and an apple. Chop them into snack-size pieces and put them into Ziploc bags so anyone can grab a healthy nibble during the week. It takes five minutes—seven max!

• Build Around Basics: Cook the same staples over and over again—and spice them up with a veggie. The more you cook something, the easier and faster it becomes. Prepare the same basics (e.g., chicken and rice, rice and beans, fish and couscous) Monday, Wednesday, and Friday, and simply add a new and different vegetable into the mix each night. It feels like you're eating something different, but the routine is the same.

• Turn on Your Crock Pot: The crock pot is an incredible invention that truly makes cooking dinner easier. Simply set it up in the morning, and when you walk in the door, dinner is ready. Visit the sites below for delicious recipes:

http://allrecipes.com/Recipes/Main-Dish/Slow-Cooker/Top.aspx

http://busycooks.about.com/od/favoritecrockpotrecipes/a/favoritecrockpo.htm

• End Multiple-Meal Madness: It's easy to get caught in the trap of thinking you have to make multiple meals to accommodate picky eaters. Kids are developing their ego/sense of self and snacks/meals are one of their pre-ferred battlegrounds. Don't engage, because you'll lose every time. The fact of the matter is kids want to mimic older children and adults, so serve them what you're having and eventually their curiosity will win the day. If a child is hungry, he'll eat anything. If he's not hungry, there's no need to force the issue. If your husband or best friend doesn't finish everything on their plate or picks around something, do you make a big deal of it? No! Why should your child be any different?

• Delegate, Delegate, Delegate:

1. Keep a running shopping list on a notepad in the kitchen so that anyone can buy the groceries during the week.

2. Have kids under ten but over age three set the table, and have kids over ten help prep the meal.

3. On Sunday afternoon, have each member of the family pick the menu for one night of the week. That's a few less meals for you to figure out *and* you'll know at least one other person will like what's for dinner that night!

4. Institute this rule: If you cook, you're off the hook for cleaning up and doing the dishes.

• Prep Staples in Advance: If you use vegetables like onions, carrots, and broccoli in a lot of different meals, pre-prep them all at once when you have time. Keep them fresh in Ziploc bags in the fridge so they're ready to go when you need them in a flash during the week. This can cut ten to twenty minutes from your nightly meal routine. If you're using browned meat or grilled chicken in a few recipes during the week, brown it/grill it when you get it home from the store and put it in the fridge so all you have to do during the week is reheat.

• Double the Recipe: Once or twice a week, double the recipe you're making. That way you'll have a meal that you can freeze and have at the ready on another night when you don't want to cook. You're making the same thing you were already, just more of it. Use the frozen meal on a night when you need a get-out-of-the-kitchen-free card.

• Go Green: You can make incredible salads in about ten minutes. Just go to the fridge, take out all the veggies you have, find a protein, cut it all up, and throw it together in a bowl. Voilà—you've got a delicious, hearty meal. If you think kids/husbands won't eat it, you're underestimating the power of ranch dressing (or the game of choosing the best salad dressing).

• Use a Pressure Cooker: When the pressure is on to get something healthy on the table pronto, use a pressure cooker. The super-heated steam, which is produced by high temperatures inside a pressure cooker, cooks food quickly, minimizes the leeching of vitamins and minerals, and intensifies the natural flavors of your food.

way to make dinner prep less overwhelming? The answer is yes. It just takes a little practice, some streamlining, and a backup plan.

- *Practice, Practice, Practice:* The people who are naturally good at preparing healthy, quick meals didn't get there overnight. They practiced making good dishes often enough that it became second nature. Start small, make up one or two healthy menus, and master each dish. Gradually add new ones to your repertoire. The next thing you know, you'll be a pro.

- *Streamline, Streamline, Streamline:* The second trick of those who magically throw together healthy meals is that they look to reduce drag anywhere they can. They streamline their what's-for-dinner process by making a plan for the week, preferably with help from others. They streamline their shopping with lists and, where available, computer ordering. They streamline their prep by having essential tools within arm's reach.

- *Prepare for Chaos:* Have a "free" night scheduled into the week, just in case. Know what your healthy backup plan is—whether it's reheating something frozen you made earlier, eating leftovers, or ordering a pizza, so you're not heading out for super-fatty fast food at the eleventh hour.

---

1. National Center for Policy Analysis, "Two Income Families Now the Norm," October 2000.

2. National Institute for Occupational Safety and Health, "Stress at Work," Publication 99-101.

3. Judith Groch. "Convenience Foods Save Little Time, Lack Nutrients," www.medpagetoday.com.

ADDITIONAL RESOURCES

PRODUCTS

Blackberry | www.na.blackberry.com
Buttoned Up Weekly Agenda | http://shopping.franklinplanner.com
iPhone | www.apple.com | 1-(800) MY-APPLE
iPod Nano | www.apple.com/ipodnano/ | 1-(800) MY-APPLE
Life.doc Kit | www.getbuttonedup.com
Palm | www.palm.com/us/
Post-its | www.3m.com/us/office/postit, White Board/Dry Erase Board
TiVo | www.tivo.com
Ziploc | www.ziploc.com

BOOKS/MAGAZINES

Checklists for Life by Kristen M. Lagatree | (New York: Random House Reference, 1999).
Everything (Almost) in Its Place by Alicia Rockmore and Sarah Welch | (New York: St. Martins, 2008); www.getbuttonedup.com.
FLIP for Decorating by Elizabeth Mayhew | (New York: Ballantine, 2009).
Happy at Work, Happy at Home by Caitlin Friedman and Kimberly Yorio. | (New York: Broadway, 2009).
It's All Too Much Workbook by Peter Walsh | (New York: Free Press, 2009).
O magazine | www.oprah.com/magazine/omagazine
Perfectly Imperfect: A Life in Progress by Lee Woodruff and Bob Woodruff | (New York: Random House, 2009).
Real Simple magazine | www.realsimple.com; 1-877-747-1048
SHED Your Stuff. Change Your Life: A Four-Step Guide to Getting Unstuck by Julie Morgenstern | (New York: Fireside, 2009).
Throw Out Fifty Things, by Gail Blanke | (New York: Springboard, 2009).

WEBSITES

Big Dates | www.bigdates.com
Blog Her | www.blogher.com
Cozi | www.cozi.com
Department of Homeland Security | www.ready.gov
eFax | www.efax.com
Evite | www.evite.com
Free Conference | www.freeconferencepro.com
Google | Services: Alerts, Chrome, Health, Docs, and Picasa, www.google.com
HGTV | www.hgtv.com

STORES/CATALOGS

Alice | www.alice.com

Amazon.com | www.amazon.com

Bed, Bath & Beyond | www.bedbathandbeyond.com

Buttoned Up, Inc. | www.getbuttonedup.com

The Container Store | www.containerstore.com

Home Shopping Network | www.hsn.com

Organize.com | www.organize.com

QVC | www.qvc.com

Target | www.target.com

Walmart | www.walmart.com

EXPERTS

Alicia Rockmore and Sarah Welch | www.getButtonedup.com | info@
getbuttonedup.com

Elizabeth Mayhew | www.elizabethmayhew.com

Jean Chatzky | www.jeanchatzky.com

Julie Morgenstern | www.juliemorgenstern.com

Mommy Tracked | www.mommytracked.com

National Association of Professional Organizers | www.napo.net

BLOGS AND TWITTER

Five Dollar Dinners | www.5dollardinners.com

From Dates to Diapers | www.fromdatestodiapers.com

Get Buttoned Up | www.getbuttonedup.com
@GetButtonedUp | @SarahButtonedUp | @Rockmore

Money Saving Mom | www.moneysavingmom.com

OTHER

1-800-Got-Junk | (800) GOT-JUNK | www.1800gotjunk.com

Buzzom | www.buzzom.com

eBay | www.ebay.com

The Knot and The Nest | www.theknot.com; www.thenest.com

Moving.com | www.moving.com

Stumble Upon | www.stumbleupon.com

Technorati | www.technorati.com

U.S. Post Office | www.usps.com

White Fence | www.whitefence.com

You Send It | www.yousendit.com

THE FIVE WE CAN'T LIVE WITHOUT

Alicia

Daily Candy | www.dailycandy.com

Facebook | www.facebook.com

Modern Mom | www.modernmom.com

Tweet Deck | www.tweetdeck.com

Web MD | www.webmd.com

Sarah

Google Reader | www.Google.com/Reader/Play

Hoot Suite | www.Hootsuite.com

Mint (financial organization) | www.Mint.com

Mobile Me | www.me.com

Online Banking Websites, such as: | www.Wachovia.com, www.BankofAmerica.com, www.Citibank.com, www.AmericanExpress.com (etc.)

Sarah Welch and Alicia Rockmore are co-founders of Buttoned Up, a company dedicated to helping busy people get organized sanely. The company offers tips and tools for getting imperfectly organized via their blog, GetButtonedUp.com, and they also have a line of stationery products available at fine retailers across the United States.

Sarah Welch identifies herself as a "yo-yo organizer." Despite her feelings of organizational inadequacy, she's a seasoned entrepreneur who is used to juggling two or more jobs and a million details at once so she can make ends meet and chase her dreams. Over the years she has learned that the secret to getting it all done is . . . well . . . not to try! Instead she focuses on maintaining momentum on all fronts with the help of the 80/20 rule (and a good sense of humor helps quite a bit too).

Prior to cofounding Buttoned Up, Sarah was a New York advertising agency executive and entrepreneur. She managed client relationships and studied what makes people tick at J. Walter Thompson, Ammirati Puris Lintas, and M&C Saatchi, then struck out on her own as a marketing consultant in 2000. She has worked with a long list of big-brand marketers, including Kellogg, Unilever, MSN, General Motors, Gap, and Bank of America. In addition to Buttoned Up, Inc., she cofounded Mindset Media, LLC. Sarah has a bachelor of science degree from Georgetown University.

Sarah and her husband, Gardiner, also a successful entrepreneur, live in Westchester County, New York, with their sons, William and Lachlan. She says, "Once you let go of the quest to become 'perfectly organized,' it's amazing how much easier (and fun) it is to get and stay organized."

Alicia Rockmore is a self-proclaimed organizational maniac who seamlessly juggles a fast-paced career and full home life. Her friends and family describe her as over-the-top organized and call on her to help them get their lives buttoned up and pulled together. This includes everything from organizing closets to managing financial information to planning a family reunion.

Prior to cofounding Buttoned Up, Inc., Alicia was a marketing whiz working for well-known brands like Wish-Bone Salad Dressing, Ragu Pasta Sauces, Total Cereals, and Wheaties. Alicia received her MBA from the University of Michigan in 1992 and her bachelor's degree in economics from Claremont McKenna College in 1987. Prior to her marketing career, Alicia was a CPA with a Big 6 accounting firm.

Alicia has a lot on her plate. She juggles a full-time career along with a busy personal life that includes her disorganized but lovable husband, Adam, their eight-year-old daughter, Lucy, and her ailing 87-year-old mother. She says: "The 80/20 principle has been a lifesaver for me. I have learned that when I handle the critical things in my life, I feel so much more relaxed. Being organized does not have to be hard. As a matter of fact, it can be fun."

INDEX